THE SCENT OF HOLINESS

Lessons from a

Women's Monastery

CONSTANTINA
R. PALMER

ANCIENT FAITH
PUBLISHING

Chesterton, Indiana

The Scent of Holiness
Lessons from a Women's Monastery

Scripture quotations are taken from the New King James Version, © 1979, 1980, 1982 by Thomas Nelson, Inc. Used by permission.

Published by   Ancient Faith Publishing
                  (formerly known as Conciliar Press)
                  A division of Anceint Faith Ministries
                  P.O. Box 748
                  Chesterton, IN 46304

Printed in the United States of America

ISBN 10: 1-936270-42-0
ISBN 13: 978-1-936270-42-2

20 19 18 17 16   11 10 9 8 7 6 5 4 3

Library of Congress Cataloging-in-Publication Data

Palmer, Constantina R., 1983-
The scent of holiness : lessons from a women's monastery / by
Constantina R. Palmer.
   p. cm.
ISBN 978-1-936270-42-2 (alk. paper)
1. Palmer, Constantina R., 1983- 2. Christian pilgrims and
pilgrimages--Greece--Thessalonike. 3. Monastic and religious life of
women--Greece--Thessalonike. 4. Monasticism and religious orders for
women--Orthodox Eastern Church. 5. St. Theodora's Monastery
(Thessalonike, Greece) I. Title.

BX382.P28 2012
271'.9819092--dc23
[B]
                     2012025870

I would like to dedicate this book to the sisters who in such a short time have given me a lifetime's worth of blessings and spiritual encouragement. Words cannot express the gratitude with which my heart yearns to thank them.

"It is said that a certain brother asked an elder, 'What shall I do, father, in order to fear God?' The elder answered, 'Go and cling to a man who fears God and from the fact that he fears Him, he will teach you to do likewise.'"[1]

Contents

FOREWORD

IN A TREATISE ENTITLED, "A comparison between a king and a monk," St. John Chrysostom writes:

> But the person who has given himself to God and who has chosen the solitary life rules over anger, and envy, and love of money, and pleasure and the other evils, ever vigilant and watchful. Having placed fear of God in command over his passions, he constantly thinks of the loftiest matters. Therefore the king and the monk rule in ways such that it is fairer to call the monk king than the one who wears purple robes, a crown, and sits on a throne. . . . And if it happens that a person is in distress . . . he bypasses the king as if he were dead and flees to the dwelling of the monks, just as someone escaping a wolf flees to the hunter who carries a sword in his hand. For prayer is to a monk what a sword is to a hunter. In fact, a sword is not so fearsome to the wolves as the prayers of the just are to the

demons. Therefore, not only do we flee to the holy monks in time of need, but even the kings themselves flee to them when they are afraid, like beggars to the house of the wealthy in times of famine.

The goal of man's creation and calling is to become like God: "So God created man in His own image" (Gen. 1:27). The virtues of humility, obedience, patience, hospitality, and chastity are virtues not only for monks, but for everyone. The difference in the way of life between the monk and the married person does not change the responsibilities each has toward God's commandments. Both strive to attain perfection, only in different ways.

In *The Scent of Holiness*, Constantina Palmer offers the reader a firsthand account of her real understanding of Orthodoxy, her life in an Orthodox country, and especially her contact with and immersion in the life of Orthodox monasticism.

Such was the impact on her of the monastic way of life—in the context of the Orthodox faith—that she felt compelled to impart the lessons she learned to everyone else. The stories she relates are a good indication that she understood the essence of monastic life. By insightful observation and discreet scrutiny, she learned precious lessons from her contact with the monastic community and its members. Immersed in the life of prayer and work of the monastics, she learned about selfless love, hospitality, and imitation of Christ. Her writings are neither theological nor catechetical, but a firsthand account of monastic life that imparts a certain joy and an invitation to explore more. This sense of joy inspires the reader to read curiously one story after another in a desire to discover more of those simple but valuable lessons; in that sense we can call her accounts catechetical.

FOREWORD

The major features of Orthodoxy are humility and love. In our troubled world, Constantina's writings show us that these virtues and others still exist; the many monks and nuns who have dedicated their lives to prayer and ascetic endeavor keep them alive. St. Isaac of Syria writes in his *Ascetical Homilies*, "Ascetic endeavor is the mother of sanctification. From sanctification the first taste of the perception of Christ's mysteries is born which is called the first stage of spiritual knowledge."

Asceticism is not only for monks and nuns, but it is a necessary element for the life of all believers who seek sanctification.

I pray Constantina's book will become a part of every Christian's library.

Mother Gabriella, Abbess,
Dormition of the Mother of God Monastery,
Rives Junction, Michigan
Feast of St. Procopius
July 8, 2012

INTRODUCTION

THERE IS A WELL-KNOWN SAYING in the Orthodox Church: Angels are a light for monastics, and monastics are a light for the world.[2] Being of the world, my husband and I not only moved to an Orthodox country to learn the Orthodox faith, but once there searched for the light that would form and inform us. It was only natural we would seek guidance from those whose lives were clearly modeled after the lives of countless saints.

I was raised Roman Catholic in a family that took its faith very seriously. From a young age, I learned from my grandmother about Christ, about the Mother of God, and to offer to God my whole life, my very person. Her pious influence was essential in forming my spiritual outlook, and I believe her prayers for my family were mercifully answered by granting us the gift of Holy Orthodoxy. But finding the Orthodox faith took some time.

My brother, sister-in-law, husband, and I converted to Anglicanism while studying for our Bachelor of Arts degrees in our home province of New Brunswick, in Atlantic Canada. At that time there was still quite a traditional stronghold in Anglicanism in the Maritime Provinces; this attracted our early-Church-focused young minds. Through the providence of God we encountered a form of Christianity that seemed to have all but disappeared in our local Roman Catholic churches.

With the guidance of our Anglican priest, we started reading the Fathers of the Church and began a fairly stringent regime of prayer. The more we read about the ascetic* lives of the early saints, the more we desired to emulate them as best we could. However, as many have come to know through personal experience, Western Christianity leaves the already malnourished soul completely starving. After four years we became increasingly disappointed with the limitations of Anglicanism. We soon came to realize that Western Christianity does not and cannot uphold the canonical and spiritual life as lived out by Christians in the early centuries of the Church. And so we began to look elsewhere.

We had heard of Eastern Orthodoxy, but we were told, "It's only for Russians and Greeks. Anglicanism and Roman Catholicism are the rightful heirs of the catholic faith in the West." This statement, whether deliberately or unintentionally false, proved an obstacle for a time—but only a time. Once my brother encountered the biography of Fr. Seraphim Rose, our ill-informed perception of the Orthodox faith turned quickly into admiration.

I immediately desired full membership in what I considered to be the fulfillment of all things I had ever loved and believed in. However, it took my husband a little more time before he also saw the Orthodox Church as the only true continuation of all that we had read and heard about. With his conversion of thought came our conversion of our life into an attempt to reflect Orthodox Christianity.

* Words marked with an asterisk are defined in the Glossary beginning on page 275.

INTRODUCTION

And so, since my husband had finished his Master's degree and we wanted to continue our studies, we moved to Greece in 2007. We enrolled in the Greek language school and afterward entered the Aristotle University of Thessaloniki to study theology. My husband began his work toward his PhD,[3] and I began working toward my Master's in Theology with a focus on iconology.* I didn't know that during my time in Greece, while taking a Master's degree at the Aristotle University of Thessaloniki, I would simultaneously be taking another degree at the "University of Monasticism."

Although I anticipated learning a lot from university, I knew there was much more to Orthodoxy than books. I had been to a couple of Orthodox monasteries before moving to Greece, and my experience there forever changed my view of the Orthodox faith. It firmly established in me the idea that faith is to be lived and expressed, not merely held and stated. After this initial taste of monastic waters, I knew I would not be properly nourished without their profound influence.

St. John Chrysostom says, "You greatly delude yourself and err, if you think that one thing is demanded from the layman and another from the monk. . . . Because all must rise to the same height; and what has turned the world upside down is that we think only the monk must live rigorously, while the rest are allowed to live a life of indolence."[4] Following this conviction, we put ourselves into an environment that would strongly contribute to our own spiritual formation.

And so I sought after the guidance, friendship, and instruction of nuns, those who are wiser than the world (1 Corinthians 1:25). I didn't anticipate learning enough to fill a book, but it turns out I knew very little and learned very much. I offer this collection of lessons so that those who have not had the opportunity to live among monastics might share in their light, "the light of the world." As St. Silouan the Athonite says, "Thanks to monastics, prayer continues unceasing on earth, and the whole world profits, for through prayer the world continues to exist; but when prayer fails the world will perish."[5]

The following stories express my experiences at a women's monastery while studying in Greece. I recorded them in order to share the great benefits I received during my many visits to the spiritual fountain of life-giving water. *The Scent of Holiness* was not written to betray the whereabouts of the monastery, nor the identity of individual monastics that live there. Although some stories actually take place at other monasteries in Northern Greece, for consistency's sake I set them all in this particular monastery to which I traveled most often. Having a student's schedule allowed for me to retreat to this picturesque fifteenth-century monastery in the mountains.

The stories and experiences I have chosen to share are not accidental. I chose to record a variety of memories concerning the holy people I met, meaningful experiences, spiritual stories, life in the monastery, and quirky mistakes I made as a foreigner. Although each story may seem unrelated to those around it, I tried my best to tie together different strains of yarn so that together they would form a knot. Thus each knot is linked to the next, and together they form the thirty-three knots that make up a small, but significant, prayer rope.* Each story presents a glimpse of the life of female monastics; bound together they stand for my prayer of thanksgiving for having had that glimpse.

There are many Orthodox spiritual books and biographies of contemporary elders* and experiences in men's monasteries. However, the unique character of women's monasticism often remains hidden. Of course "there is neither male nor female" (Gal. 3:28) in Christ Jesus, but at the same time female monasticism has a distinctive quality. I think the spiritual height of women can easily be overlooked because they are not priests, nor confessors in the strict meaning of the word. And so they manage to live a much more secret life than do many elders. That does not mean, however, that some have not reached the spiritual heights of great elders. An abbess once told me, "Men try to cut the rope with an axe in one blow, while women slowly work away at severing it. In other words, men usually try to cut off their passions* with violence right from the beginning, while women try to fight their passions consistently, but gradually."

The monk and the nun will each, God willing, reach the same goal. However, the road they take may vary a little. Just as each family has its own rhythm, so does each monastery. In women's monasteries life is more or less the same as in men's, only I would say there are a few more tears, a bit more laughter, and a lot more food (for guests). Although the Father of lights is the source of every good and perfect gift (James 1:17) for both men and women, I hope that in the pages that follow, the deep, penetrating faith and spirituality specific to women will become clear. They may live more unknown lives than most monks, but their self-denial and eagerness to take up Christ's cross and follow Him are much the same. The spiritual father of this sisterhood once said, "If women were allowed on Mount Athos,* the whole mountain would be full of nuns and there would be no room left for monks!"

I once asked the abbess at this monastery about the demons: what their ranks were, were there certain demons for certain passions, and if she could explain some things about them to me. Her response was, "It's better for us to think and talk about the angels." I have tried to honor this way of thinking by focusing on the positive aspects of my experiences. I have mostly recorded my own good reactions and positive reception to the environment and those around me. It would be an oversight, however, for me not to mention that visitors to monasteries do not always have positive experiences. There are a variety of reasons for this, but most notably it is because when we visit monasteries and seek advice and help from those who are more spiritual than ourselves, the evil one fights us harder for tending to our spiritual lives.

I have consciously avoided stories that would only reveal my sins and bad thoughts and those of others. One can benefit from knowing about others' trials and temptations, but I feel it is safer to avoid scrutinizing and revealing our sins and passions to an audience. Whether our bad experiences were a result of our own actions, those of others, or merely temptations, these things are better left confessed, repented of, and forgotten.

I mention this here because I do not want my readers to feel alienated if they have had negative experiences at a monastery. Where there are struggling Christians, there is also the evil one keeping vigil. This, however, should not become a stumbling block to visiting monasteries. Monasteries are spiritual battle grounds; when we step into them, we may also be dragged into the fight. The positive lessons and experiences, though, and the holy people we meet are worth suffering through a little temptation. I wanted to present to you the spiritual fruit I was blessed to eat of while visiting such a battle ground. It is my sincere prayer and hope that someone else may benefit, even just a small amount, in the way I have benefited. This is my attempt to repay the good that was done to me.

By visiting monasteries, I believe I learned more about Christ, the Church, people, passions, spiritual victories, and myself than I could have in any other place. These lessons will not be easily forgotten. Just as one's clothes sometimes smell of incense after being in church for a long service, so my thoughts, words, and actions have retained the scent of monasticism. Just as different aromas go by different names, so does the "incense" of monasticism. It is called "love," "dedication," "obedience," "humility," "self-sacrifice," "prayer," "peace," "forgiveness," "friendship," "tears," and "laughter." Ultimately, it is the scent of holiness.

Sister Theologia often asked me, "What theology do you learn here? All we do is put you to work."

My answer is: Let me tell you what I've learned.

1

KNOT ONE

First Trip to the Monastery: Forever Home

IT WAS TRIODION* SEASON. My husband and I had only been living in Greece since October. We had enrolled in the Greek Language program in November, and my Greek was poor to nonexistent. I took a bus to a village near a women's monastery my godmother suggested I visit. There I handed a taxi driver a note with the monastery's name and address on it. He nodded, I climbed into the taxi, and we were off.

Driving through the rather large village, I noticed how much it looked like Thessaloniki—but on a small scale. It had apartment buildings, stores lining the streets, and a few beautiful Orthodox churches. As we made our way outside the village, we approached the foot of a mountain.

The taxi did not stop once we reached the main road on top of the

---

mountain, as I expected it would. I took in the most magnificent view of the surrounding mountains. Occasionally we would drive by flocks of sheep, goats, or some cows. We drove past a little house in a small valley where I later learned an old woman lived and tended her goats.

Before I knew it, the taxi was descending. We were winding down into a low valley. It seemed as though we were going all the way down to the foot of the mountain. My stomach had that nearly nauseating feeling of excitement mixed with nervousness. As we pulled into the area just in front of the monastery, I saw a nun hurrying to a building nearby. I wondered who she was.

The driver finally stopped in front of a huge metal door, and I stepped out of the taxi. There was a fountain with water coming out of a beast's mouth, and the driver went over to fill up some empty bottles. "It's a blessing,"* he said, smiling.

Many Greeks, although secular in many ways, still have a firm faith inside them and consider anything given to them from a monastery to be a blessing. This made a deep impression on my Western mind. It struck me that the almost natural cynicism in people like me can often keep us from seeing the worth of simple things. In my experience, Greeks, by contrast, receive things (especially from monasteries) in simplicity and with much more gratitude than would come naturally to me.

I paid the driver, took out my head scarf, put on my backpack, walked to the large metal door at the entrance, bent low to touch the ground, and crossed myself: "Glory to Thee, O God." I was entering the house of a saint.

What I beheld on the other side of that large door was nothing I had expected. It was the most beautiful scene I had ever laid eyes on. Everything in the courtyard looked well kept and cared for with much love. There was a fountain in the center, as in many Orthodox monasteries, and trees and plants everywhere. Some buildings looked brand new, with fresh beige walls, red trim around the curved windows, and quaint balconies the length of each floor. Others were old wooden structures that looked as if they hadn't been used in years. Stone work lined the outside of one of the buildings, creating a nice flowerbed.

Directly across the courtyard from the main gate was an intricately carved stone arch leading down some stairs and into what I later found out were workrooms. In the far distance, I could see the mountain peaks on the other side of the valley and hear the soft rumble of the waterfall just beyond the monastery wall. The air was permeated with peace. Looking back, I know the grace of the monastery enhanced its beauty.

The nuns knew I was coming, and so I looked for a bookstore to go into and introduce myself. Unfortunately, I could not see anything that looked like a bookstore. I walked across the courtyard and into the open door of the sixteenth-century church. It was dark inside. Since the monastery is in the mountains, the sun sets much faster there.

A nun was sitting near the door, so I tried to speak to her. *Tried* is the key word here. I could barely string a sentence together in Greek, and she, clearly, could barely make out a word. But in order to identify myself, I managed to mention who my godmother was and that when she comes to Greece each summer she visits this monastery. That, at least, I knew the nun understood because she repeated my godmother's name. She brought me into the nave of the church and got me to sit in one of the wooden *stasidia** along the wall. I understood a service was about to begin.

Shortly after I sat down, a nun stepped up to the chanter stand and, with a thin beeswax candle in her left hand, began reading the service of the Ninth Hour.* A little later two more nuns in flowing monastic robes took her place and started to chant: *"Kyrie ekarason pros se eisakouson mou* . . . Lord, I have cried out unto Thee. Hear Thou me, O Lord . . . *proshes tin foni tis dei se os mou* . . . give ear to the voice of my supplication, when I cry out unto Thee."

I stood motionless, listening to the most striking voices I had ever heard. I had been to other monasteries, but I had never heard chanting this beautiful. Tears began to blur my vision; I was very moved by such awe-inspiring prayer. Once Vespers* was over, the nun I had met at the door told another sister something about getting someone to come to meet me. I couldn't understand her very well, so I just stood in the narthex* looking at the few icons I could make out by the light of the lamp. The next thing I knew, the nun I had seen when the taxi entered the parking lot was there, offering her hand for me to shake.

"Hi, I'm Sarah," she said in perfect English.

Even after living in Greece for only five months, it felt comforting to hear someone speak English without a Greek accent and to shake someone's hand the way North Americans do, not just lightly while kissing cheeks in the Greek fashion.

Sr. Sarah speaks English because she grew up in Western Europe. She came to the monastery when she was about twenty-five years old. I didn't know at that time that she would become one of the closest friends I have ever had, nor that the monastery would forever take up residence in my heart.

Being Brought In

SR. SARAH AND I WALKED into a stone-floored gallery in the main wing of the monastery. Besides the main door leading into this room, there were seven other doors leading away into different rooms. It was winter, so all the doors were closed to keep the heat of the wood stove in the gallery.

Sr. Sarah opened one door that led to the kitchen. "Sit here. I'll be back in a moment."

Not a moment passed before she came back out; I stood up.

"We're not sure yet where we're going to put you. Just a second," she said, walking across the room and entering another door. I sat down.

A few more seconds and again she came out; again I stood up. She went back into the kitchen; I sat down. She came back out; I stood up.

"You don't have to stand up every time I come into the room!" she said, laughing.

Although I had visited other monasteries, I was still not sure of the proper etiquette in the presence of a monastic. I did some things out of piety, not knowing how quirky they appeared.

She led me down a long corridor into an adjoining building and into the first room on the right. It was one of the larger guest rooms, she told me. I could put my stuff down; I was going to sleep there.

"I have to run off to finish some work now, but we'll chat later," she said, closing the door behind her.

A Surprising Conversation

DURING ONE OF MY FIRST visits to the monastery, I was sitting with Sr. Sarah in the guest room, and to my amusement she told me, "You know, you don't speak with a Canadian accent."

"Well, this is how Canadians speak!" I said, laughing.

She told me a bit about her background, and I told her a bit of mine. She kept reassuring me that since I was in the guest room I could take off my headscarf, but again out of piety (and more so, ignorance)

I wasn't sure when I should take it off. "No, that's okay; I like wearing it. I even wear it around my house sometimes," I told her.

Looking back I laugh. But at the time I felt so stupid for saying that. I did a lot of things out of zeal when I first became Orthodox, but it didn't take long for my zeal to cool off. Zeal is a wonderful gift from God—zeal combined with discernment is even better. But I learned that I should have struggled with all my might to keep that zeal, even in its raw stages, because undoubtedly the day comes when we wake up and it's gone, and then our Christian struggle becomes much more difficult.

While we were chatting, a nun whom the sisters lovingly called *Yia-yia** came in looking for her jacket. The room I was staying in had once been a storage room. So she had the habit, formed some years prior, of leaving her jacket there.

Yia-yia, whose monastic name was Paraskevi, was very old and walked slowly with a slight slouch. She was mumbling to herself and drying her hands on her skirt.

Sr. Sarah told me, "This is Yia-yia. She has Alzheimer's. She never wipes her hands on the hand towel in the bathroom, because when she was young it grossed her out to use the same towel that everyone else used. Now that she has lost her memory, she has reverted to this bad habit. This is why Gerontissa* always tells us, '*Stomen kalo, stomen meta fovou*'—'Let us stand well, let us stand with fear'—meaning, we should be careful while we're young not to keep bad habits because they'll come back to us when we're older."

Just as Sr. Sarah was finishing this tidbit of information, Yia-yia handed her a jacket. "Is this mine?"

"No, Yia-yia. I'll get it for you." Sr. Sarah got up and walked over to the closet, which still held a few spare jackets—including Yia-yia's.

Sr. Sarah helped Yia-yia put her jacket on. "This is Constantina,

Yia-Yia. She converted to Orthodoxy and was just baptized not even a year ago," she said, gesturing in my direction.

"Welcome," Yia-yia said. Quickly glancing at Sr. Sarah she asked, "What's my name?"

"Paraskevi," Sr. Sarah answered.

"Paraskevi," Yia-yia repeated, stretching her hand out toward me.

What happened next took me completely by surprise. She looked back at Sr. Sarah and, speaking about me, said, "She was different before her baptism. She was only for crying, but now, now she has joy."

Sr. Sarah translated just as Yia-yia finished speaking. Yia-yia then turned and walked out of the room, leaving me sitting with my mouth open and my eyes glistening with tears.

"It's true," I said to Sr. Sarah in a voice that betrayed my astonishment.

"Yia-yia is very spiritual and has prayer of the heart.* That's how she knew that," Sr. Sarah responded, her eyes also welling up.

Yia-yia's gift of prayer of the heart became obvious at other times. But those stories are best saved for later.

2

KNOT TWO

My First Lesson

THE FIRST TIME I MET the abbess, she was sitting outside the kitchen cutting up broccoli. I was intimidated by her, because she was an abbess, because of the language barrier, and even because she was so tall for a Greek. I bowed and touched the ground, she held out her right hand, and I kissed it—this is the customary way of taking a blessing, not only from an abbess, but from a priest or bishop as well. She gestured for me to sit down and in her soft voice asked me about where I was from, how long I was going to be in Greece, et cetera. Fortunately, there was a nun who spoke English working nearby, and she helped interpret.

"Gerontissa" is the title used by monastics and laypeople to address an abbess. It literally means "old woman," but strictly speaking it is reserved for holy women who possess the gift of spiritual direction. The abbess's monastic name was Philareti, which means "lover of virtue," and she was worthy of both names.

While we were speaking, Sr. Epomoni (which means "patience") carried in some packages from the mail to open in front of the abbess. The packages were filled with black jackets. Sr. Epomoni took them out to see how they fit. They looked a little small. She tried on the largest size, and still the sleeves ended about two or three inches above her wrists. More nuns came out of different rooms, and noticing the jackets, came over to see them. One of the smallest nuns tried one on, and it barely fit. Giggling ensued. Sr. Epomoni looked at me smiling.

"We ordered these from America and they sent the wrong sizes."

Instead of being frustrated or even slightly annoyed, the nuns found an opportunity to smile and laugh at the inconvenience of having thirty or more jackets that did not fit them.

"We'll just have to send them back," Sr. Epomoni said.

Lesson number one was completed. No one complained, no one groaned, no one got angry or blamed anyone. They just laughed a lot and then shrugged, as if to say, "Oh well," and as quickly as they came out to see what had come in the mail, they were back to work.

Many Who Are First Will Be Last

THE FIRST DIVINE LITURGY I attended at the monastery was during my first visit. Early in the morning I heard the faint sound of a *talanton** and a *symandron** before finally hearing the familiar sound of church bells. The Divine Liturgy was about to begin, just after the First Hour finished. I got dressed and went to the church.

Some of the nuns sit in a segregated section of the church, while others sit in the nave, so I wasn't sure where I should sit. That's how I made my third error. I went into the nave and sat down in the stasidi the nun directed me to sit in the first evening I arrived. I didn't know that it was reserved for the "second in command" of the monastery, nor did I know that it was next to the stasidi of Gerontissa Philareti.

When Gerontissa came in and stood in front of her stasidi I blushed and felt very embarrassed that I had presumed to sit in a place so close to the abbess. But, of course, no one told me to move or made me feel remotely uncomfortable. I only realized when I saw Sr. Paisia standing there the next day—and at each subsequent Liturgy—that it was reserved for someone far more important than myself.

The service was very beautiful. It was serene, orderly, and illumined by oil lamps and candlelight. Since the day was dawning, the gradual ascent of the sun made the beauty of the church more visible. I was blown away by the intricately carved iconostasis* and the beauty of the icons. A local bishop had donated an icon of Christ the Pantocrator* to the monastery many years ago. It was painted in the fourteenth century, and it made a particular impression on me. It is said that Christ's eyes appear to watch you wherever you may be standing in the church.

After taking in all the sights in the old church, I returned to the room I was staying in. There, already all laid out, was the sweetest little breakfast. I particularly remember being impressed with the way the napkin was folded. The napkin made a sleeve which had the utensils tucked into it.

Helping Hindered by Greek Hospitality

AFTER BREAKFAST I WANTED TO HELP with work, but it is not as common in Greece for pilgrims to help with work at a monastery as it is in North America. Most Greeks go to monasteries to have a coffee and a sweet, light a candle or two, venerate icons, and look through the bookstore. So I didn't have much success trying to persuade the nuns to let me help.

"Sr. Joanna, can I help with something in the kitchen?"

"Ah . . . I'll have to ask . . . Maybe you would like a coffee instead?"

"Um, okay, thanks."

I didn't really want a coffee—at least not a *Greek* coffee. But I tried to have a Greek mindset. *It's a blessing*, I told myself.

She brought me in a coffee accompanied by a glass of water and three cookies on a tray: typical Greek monastic hospitality.

Once I finished, I took my dishes into the kitchen. Then I looked around at the small library they have for the guests in the reception room. Half an hour passed. Sr. Akakia came into the room.

"Sister, can I help with anything?"

"Why don't you have a coffee?"

"I had one, thanks."

"Well, perhaps you'd like some ice cream?"

"No thanks, Sister."

The nuns were reluctant to let me help, because when pilgrims visit the monastery, the nuns want them to feel as though they are on retreat from their work and responsibilities in the world. Since it was my first visit, it wasn't hospitable—in their opinion—to put me to work. It didn't take long, though, for them to get to know me, and after a few more visits they willingly took me up on my offer to help.

As weeks turned into months and months turned into years, I received many a phone call from the sisters requesting my help—and even that of my husband. It was always a pleasure to go to the monastery and work alongside them. The fact that I learned something new and interesting each time I went was just a bonus.

That They Might Arrive at the Measure of Perfection

AS A PART OF THE Orthodox baptismal service, during the exorcism prayers, the priest asks the candidate, "Do you renounce Satan and all his works?" To which the candidate responds, "I renounce Satan and all his works." Then the priest asks, "Do you join yourself to Christ?" and the candidate answers, "I join myself to Christ." This exchange of renouncing and resolving is very similar to the monastic tonsure.* The candidate approaches the monastic life without coercion or necessity, but simply out of an honest love and desire to join Christ and to turn from Satan and all his works.

In the Greek tradition, a monastic will usually go through two tonsures, that to rassophore (literally, "rasso-wearer") and, God willing, another into the great schema.* Tonsure as a stavrophore (or the small schema) happens far less frequently in contemporary practice in Greek monasteries. The ultimate goal, however, is for all monastics to "cultivate the grace they received and multiply and increase the talent of their Lord, namely, the spiritual strength which the divine schema mystically granted their soul, through struggle against the demons, through conquering the passions, and through the charismata which they will receive from the Holy Spirit."[6]

I was blessed to be one among hundreds to attend the tonsure of the sisterhood's novices into rassophore status. Of their own free will they were clothed in the black habit of renouncement of the pleasures of this life, just as the angel revealed it to St. Pachomius (the exception being they don't receive the *analavos** of the great schema).

It was the evening of the fourth of January, and I wondered if, when Gerontissa Philareti decided it was time for the novices to be tonsured, she consciously chose to have the service take place during the Vespers for the feast of St. Syncletike.

St. Syncletike is like the St. Anthony the Great of female monasticism. She, like St. Anthony, was also a "professor of the desert"; she was an ascetic, a teacher, an abbess, a writer, and suffered like a martyr. She is a wonderful example not only for nuns and monks to look to, but for all struggling Christians seeking instruction from one whose wisdom surpasses that of the world.

I stood at the back of the nave, next to St. Syncletike's icon as well as the festal icon of the Nativity of Christ. They held the service in the main church on account of the large crowd, whereas they would normally have had Vespers in the small chapel. In fact, there were so many people in front of me that although I was taller than most, even on my tiptoes I could only see the bishop standing at the royal doors.* The four novices stood in front of him. I heard him say, "If any man will come after Me, let him deny himself, and take up his cross daily and follow Me." He said it three times. And before I knew it he was holding scissors and announcing the new name of each nun as he cut each one's hair. Just as in baptism, so again in their monastic tonsure the sisters had very small portions of their hair cut, first in the front, then in the back, then from the right, and finally from the left—making the sign of the cross.

I didn't expect the service to be so short, since next to nothing is short when it comes to services in the Orthodox Church, but I also didn't expect the atmosphere to be so full of joy and peace. And there was not only joy and peace, but an inexpressible feeling that I was witnessing something unique. Orthodox monasticism is completely radical. These women were willingly taking upon themselves a lifestyle completely contrary to our sin-inclined nature, and yet entirely befitting our first-intended nature.

We were created to be like monastics, to worship God with all our attention, in every facet of our daily lives—to take up our cross and follow Him. From the beginning we have been called to renounce Satan and all his works, to renounce our passions, sins, self-will; to renounce our high opinion of ourselves, our self-justification, our judgmental thoughts. We were intended to put on the robe of righteousness, just as the sisters put on their black habits that symbolize death to the world. We will each go about it in different ways, but go about it we must.

As the Vespers service finished, I reflected on the newly tonsured nuns. They had waited years for this moment. They had struggled and fought temptations, passions, bad thoughts, and here they were at the true beginning of their monastic life. Things would become harder, but also sweeter. There would be periods of grace and periods of difficult temptations, as St. Syncletike herself taught:

> Those who put out to sea at first sail with a favorable wind; then the sails spread, but later the wind becomes adverse. Then the ship is tossed by the waves and is no longer controlled by the rudder. But when in a little while there is calm, and the tempest dies down, then the ship sails on again. So it is with us, when we are driven by the spirits who are against us; we hold to the cross as our sail and so we can set a safe course.[7]

The sisters' potential victories and failures would now be on a higher level. They were no longer laywomen, but monastics; no longer novices, but enlisted as front-line soldiers in the Christian army. But, as our mother of the desert said, they have the cross to hold to, which will guide them safely in their battles.

KNOT TWO

After the archimandrite* who accompanied the bishop chanted, "Through the prayers of the holy bishop, Lord Jesus Christ our God, have mercy on us and save us. Amen," the sisters turned to face the crowd. Clothed in their habits, they stood in front of the church while we all greeted them one by one. We wished them "good obedience," and a "good Paradise," and asked their names: Sisters Margaret, Monica, Marina, and Thekla. Now dedicated to Christ their Bridegroom in a way they were not before, their faces bore a new illumination, a new joy, a new resolve to cut off their wills and live in obedience and humility until they, with the help of the life-giving and saving Cross, certainly and safely finish the battle which was set before them on that very evening, during the Vespers service of St. Syncletike, the mother of monasticism.

KNOT THREE

Forgiveness Sunday

THE EVENING BEFORE CLEAN MONDAY* saw the church filled with faithful from the nearby village. It was Forgiveness Sunday,* and we were starting off Great Lent with a long but beautiful Vespers service. I received a blessing to record the service, and I still enjoy listening to it. One of the most memorable parts of that experience was when Sr. Euphemia came around censing with the *katzio** while they chanted, "Let my prayer be set forth as incense before Thee."

Everyone stood (as best as they were able in the pressing crowd) while Sr. Euphemia slowly made her way through, censing both icons and laity. She was like a shadow lost in the darkness of the church, only distinguishable by the chiming of the bells and the light reflecting off the censer she was holding. By the time she maneuvered through the crowd to me, they were chanting, "For unto Thee, O Lord, O Lord, are mine eyes, in Thee have I hoped." I bowed low as the incense filled my senses.

Once the service ended, all the nuns, following the abbess, venerated the icons, took her blessing, and one after the other added to the line of nuns until each sister had asked forgiveness of every other. Then the laity in turn venerated, took Gerontissa's blessing, and bowed to each nun. I still didn't know the sisters very well, and so their actions as I went down the line to exchange requests for forgiveness surprised me. Some said my name with voices full of emotion; others drew me close to hug me, and still others even kissed my hand.

The mood was somber, but strangely light-hearted. We were beginning a journey—a long journey, but one we would travel together. There were many exclamations of well wishes: "Good struggle!" and "Have a good forty days!" I left the church more compunctionate over my sins than when I had entered, but also more prepared to set out with determination on the long trek to Golgotha, encouraged that I would not be ascending alone.

The Grace of the Martyrs

ONE AFTERNOON I WAS WITH Sr. Euphemia in the bakery, tending to some freshly baked bread. I asked her, "Sister, how did you decide to become a nun at *this* monastery?"

"I knew since I was young that I wanted to become a monastic, but I thought I was going to go to a monastery just outside Thessaloniki. But the first time I visited this monastery, I felt such a strong presence of the Holy Spirit around me that I just knew I had to stay here. I knew I was called to become a monastic *here*."

"I also find that I feel different in this place than I do in other monasteries," I told her. "I didn't realize this until I visited a monastery on one of the Greek islands. I thought that monastery would be my favorite because I had heard so much about it and had seen pictures of how beautiful it was. But a few days after our trip to that monastery, some friends and I came here, and immediately as we drove down the hill, I started feeling that overwhelming sense of warmth and peace that the monastery often emanates. I felt that I was home. When we arrived, I asked Sr. Hara why I felt that way and in her soft voice she said, 'The monastery had so many monastics live here throughout the years and many martyrs as well. It's the grace of the martyrs that makes you feel that way.'"

The exact number of martyred monastics at the monastery is not known. However, we do know that a good number of them were killed at the hands of foreign Muslims. A little over one hundred years ago, Muslims from a country bordering Greece came to pillage the monastery. Before killing the nuns, they searched all over for valuable items to take with them. At that time there was an older man from the nearby village who helped take care of the church. When the Muslims entered the church, they threatened the sacristan* in order to coerce him to tell them where the finest treasures of the monastery were held. He, unbeknownst to the Muslims, was standing in front of a concealed door behind which the treasures were hidden. However, he vehemently refused to reveal the location of the monastery's most prized possessions, and so the Muslims beat him to death, right there in the church, in front of the secret door. To this day, this man's descendants still live in the nearby village.

Then the Muslims took what they were able to find—mostly historical, original manuscripts from the monastery's library—and killed the nuns, some by placing them in boiling tar. And so they gave up their souls to the glory of God. By the grace of God, and so we would know the account of their martyrdom, one nun escaped and shared the martyrs' story. Their grace now rests in the monastery, the "place of their repentance." May we have their blessing!

The Great Canon of St. Andrew of Crete

ON CLEAN MONDAY MORNING, before I left to return to Thessaloniki, I joined the nuns in the church for the Great Canon of St. Andrew of Crete.* I couldn't seem to find a seat that didn't have a nun within five feet of me, so I went to the stasidi furthest away from the nearest nun. Unfortunately for me, that meant going to the very front of the church, in front of all the nuns. This was fine until it came to the point where everyone started doing continuous prostrations.

I was mortified. Just a month prior to this I was diagnosed with arthritis, and since the swelling in my knees was still quite serious, I did bows instead of prostrations. That would have been fine if no one could see me. But as it was, since I was in front of all the nuns, I was embarrassed to only bow, while they were doing full prostrations (and quickly, too). I grimaced every time I bent to touch the ground.

They must think you're so lazy, I thought to myself. *Of all the places to stand, I had to be in front of all the nuns!*

What I didn't realize then, due to the blindness of my vanity, is that no one would ever have taken notice of what I was doing. They were too busy doing what they were supposed to be doing to worry about me. Knowing them the way I do now, I know that *if* they took note of me they probably thought something like, *Oh, look at Constantina doing all those bows, she's from the world and struggles . . . What do I do?*

4

KNOT FOUR

Archimandrite Evsevios Vittis

THIS HOLY ELDER, may his memory be eternal, used to visit Gerontissa and the sisterhood when he was alive. He was a well-known hermit who lived in Northern Greece, renowned for his wisdom and spiritual insight. He had both divine and acquired gifts. He spoke many foreign languages and wrote even more books.

In his earlier years he had immigrated to Sweden. Seeing the spiritual hunger of the people there, especially the Greek immigrants, he was ordained to the holy priesthood. In 1973 he established a skete* for himself in the Swedish woods: the Hesychastarion* of St. Nicolas in Ratrik.

While living in the skete, he supported himself by working as a humble custodian. After some time he became so well known that a steady stream of letters addressed to him started pouring into the skete. He was a light on a hilltop for Orthodox Christians everywhere. However, at the urging of his spiritual father, he returned to Greece in 1980 and retreated to the Skete of Faya Petra in Sidirokastro in Northern Greece, a dependency of the holy monastery of Grigoriou on Mount Athos. His spiritual light grew ever stronger and shone brightly in his homeland.

He died in 2009 at the age of eighty-two. In accordance with his humility, he did not wish for his death and burial to be made known to the public. He wanted a few fathers from the monastery of Grigoriou on the Holy Mountain* to bury him simply. Yet out of love and devotion to the elder, the fathers permitted hierarchs to come. And although they did not announce it to the public, hundreds of faithful managed to make their way to the funeral.

While he was still alive, I had heard of him from friends in Thessaloniki. They told me there was a clairvoyant elder living in Northern Greece, not far from Thessaloniki, who spoke a variety of languages and was known for curing people of cancer, among other things.

They told me about a woman who had cancer and went to see the elder, hoping he would cure her of her illness. They spoke together and he told her to confess. She said she had confessed. But to her surprise, the elder told her if she didn't confess a particular sin she had committed, then the cancer would not go away. Sure enough, she confessed and was healed.

I was very enthused when I heard this story and asked where he lived and if we could go and see him. They told me he lived in Sidirokastro in a skete, but that he often did not receive visitors. Having neither a car nor knowledge of the way there, I let it go; I wouldn't meet the elder any time soon—or so I thought.

About two months after that conversation, I was staying at the monastery and working with Sr. Sarah in the bookstore. I had gone to get something, and on my return Sr. Silouani asked me, "Do you know who is coming tonight?"

"No. Who?" I asked.

"Elder Evsevios," she said.

"Who is that?"

"He's a living saint. He works miracles—I've told you about him in the past. He is coming sometime after we close the gate and will speak with us in the gathering room," she whispered.

Once the visitors had left the bookstore, we packed up and went over to the kitchen. All the nuns were busy finishing up their work so they would be ready to sit and hear the elder when he arrived. I started asking Sr. Xenia about who the elder was. When she told me, "He probably speaks English since he knows a lot of languages," my mouth dropped open.

"He speaks many languages?" I asked in amazement.

"Yes," she answered.

"Is he the hermit who lives north of Thessaloniki?"

"He is a hermit and does live north of Thessaloniki."

"And he cures people from cancer?"

"Yes," she said, smiling.

"Oh my goodness, I didn't know *that* was who Sr. Silouani was talking about!"

In the past Sr. Silouani had told me some things about this elder, but I had never made the connection that he was the elder I had heard about from my friends.

I became so excited I could hardly contain myself. I continued putting dishes away, but when I saw Sr. Sarah and Sr. Thekla, I started explaining how I had heard of the elder before, how he had cured a woman from cancer, and the other things I had heard about.

"Make the sign of the cross, Constantina," Sr. Thekla calmly suggested.

"Why?" I asked in bewilderment.

"Because you are very excited and the devil sees everything," she said simply.

I made the sign of the cross and struggled to better contain my enthusiasm. I had heard of this before—not expressing your emotions too outwardly so as not to give the evil one more ground than he needs in tempting you. But I must say, this did strike me as a little odd at first.

However, it is more spiritually prudent to be measured when expressing any outward signs of emotion. This way the evil one has less ammunition, since he can only judge our thoughts and feelings based on what we externally reveal to him. He can neither see the future nor read our thoughts. Abba Arsenios describes it in this way: "The unclean spirits are capable of understanding the quality of our thoughts and *logismoi*,* not because they can penetrate into the soul, but rather because they carefully observe certain of our outward expressions or bodily movements."[8]

And so temperance in displaying sadness, anger, frustration, hurt, and even enthusiasm guards us against the evil one's wiles and temptations. As for the elder's visit and the lessons I learned from him, they will have to come later.

Through the Prayers . . .

SR. SERAPHIMA CAME INTO the kitchen after working in the garden. While she was washing her hands, I asked her, "Were you and the other sisters able to finish the work you needed to get done in the garden?"

"Through the prayers," was her response.

I was perplexed by this answer. I knew this common phrase from the prayer that is always said at the end of all Orthodox services— "Through the prayers of our Holy Fathers, Lord Jesus Christ our God, have mercy on us"—but I was not sure why she was saying it in response to my question. I thought about it for some time. I could understand a "Glory to God," but this phrase seemed somehow out of place to me.

While drying the dishes and pondering this, it suddenly struck me. *Of course! Not just "Through the prayers" but "Through the prayers of the* Holy Fathers"! She was attributing the work they were able to accomplish not to the sisters' own strength, but to the strength that was given to them through the prayers of the Holy Fathers.

After this, I started viewing my own work and successes in a different light. This phrase found much more frequent use in my own speech. By saying this simple phrase, Sr. Seraphima showed me the importance of viewing all that we do as being not merely for the glory of God, but because someone is praying for us.

Laughter

THE FIRST TIME MY HUSBAND accompanied me to the monastery, we enjoyed having a tour and getting to know the nuns better. Although we were becoming more comfortable around monastics, we were both still a little unsure of how we should act. Laughter, for instance, we thought would be inappropriate. Laughter in moderation, it turns out, is quite helpful in keeping life in the monastery healthy and manageable.

I was often the *cause* of laughter, which I gladly accepted because I loved to see the nuns laugh. Their laughter made me laugh even harder, as after the all-night vigil on the Leave-taking* of Pascha.*

The nuns had prepared the traditional Paschal soup, *magiritsa*, for after the Divine Liturgy, since the Leave-taking was like a second Pascha. Because monastics abstain from meat all year round, the nuns prepared this delicious soup with seafood instead of the regular lamb's intestines (for which I was very thankful).

We were walking across the courtyard, heading toward the guest house, and Sr. Sarah told me, "You and John will eat dinner with Sr. Lydia's grandmother and grandfather. You'll be shocked how young her grandfather looks!" This is what I *heard*; that is not what she said.

While we were eating, I tried hard not to laugh at *just* how young her grandfather looked. I just couldn't get over how much younger the grandfather looked than his wife. She looked at least twenty years older. While we were eating, Mrs. Sevasti (the grandmother) peeled his boiled egg for him, cut it up, put salt and pepper on it, filled his glass full of water, and made sure he had enough bread to eat—just as most Greek moms do for their sons.

All the while I watched, nearly dying, trying to control my laughter at the thought that it was her husband. I couldn't wait to tell John.

We finished eating, stood up, and said the prayer of thanksgiving, and John and I returned to our room.

"John, you're not going to believe this, but that was Sr. Lydia's grandfather!"

"No, you're wrong, that can't be her grandfather."

"Sr. Sarah told me he looked young," I insisted.

"You must have misunderstood her," he responded.

"I'll prove it to you; I'll go ask Sr. Sarah."

I figured I might catch her in the kitchen since the nuns were also eating the traditional Pascha soup in their dining hall. The nuns had just finished eating and were bringing their dishes out.

"Sr. Sarah, was that Sr. Lydia's grandfather?" I asked.

"What? No! It was her *uncle!*"

"I thought you said they were her grandparents, and that her grandfather looked young."

"No! I said her *grandmother* looked young!"

"Oh, well that makes a lot more sense. I was trying very hard not to laugh while eating with them, thinking they were a married couple!"

We parted laughing. I returned to my room, and she returned to the *trapeza.** About ten minutes later, I went into the kitchen to get some water. As soon as Sr. Marina saw me, she placed one hand over her mouth and one hand across her stomach, trying to contain her laughter. The other nuns in the kitchen joined in laughing. Laughter is always contagious, especially around women, especially in the middle of the night.

Sr. Sarah said, "I told the sisters you thought Sr. Lydia's uncle was her grandfather, and Sr. Raphaela asked if I had told you in Greek who you would be eating with. When I told them, 'No, I told her in *English*,' they lost it!"

Our laughter gradually died down and we said good night. As I was walking back to my room, sporadic, stifled laughter could still be heard from the kitchen.

John jokingly remarked afterwards, "Oh great, we come to a monastery and you make everybody lose it!"

That was my introduction to the light-hearted side these nuns had.

5

KNOT FIVE

For the Kingdom of Heaven's Sake

S R. SILOUANI NEVER ANTICIPATED becoming a nun. Although faithful, she, like many people, lived for fine clothing and pleasant décor to put in her home. She was married to a faithful man, but they were unable to have children. This grieved them very much, and so they decided to speak with their spiritual father about adopting. He advised them against this—not as a rule (for he advised friends of theirs to do this very thing), but simply not in their case. So they continued to pray to the Mother of God and various other saints, asking for their intercession to conceive a child. They even went to the famous church of the Annunciation of the Theotokos* on the island of Tinos, surrounded by the Aegean, east of Athens.

Tinos is a central place of pilgrimage for those suffering from all forms of ailments and for women unable to conceive. The miraculous icon housed in the church is called "Great Grace," and it is to this likeness of the Theotokos that people flock to ask for her intercession. The icon was found after the Mother of God appeared to a nun and told her of its location. Although it is named after the Feast of the Annunciation, the church's primary feast is celebrated on the Feast of the Dormition on August 15, on which day thousands of people visit from all over Greece and other countries.

Sr. Silouani later told me she refused to leave the church after Vespers so she could stay there all night before the Divine Liturgy started in the morning. However, despite their fervent prayers, God had another plan for them, it seemed.

After years of tears and prayers for them to be granted a child, Sr. Silouani and her husband accepted the will of the all-good God for them to remain childless. With the blessing of their spiritual father, they agreed to live as brother and sister for the rest of their lives.

Their faith continued to grow, but especially that of Sr. Silouani's husband, until he was eventually reading the daily cycle of services of the Orthodox Church each day. He would rise and read Matins,* throughout the day he would read the Hours, and in the evening he would say Vespers or go to the parish nearby, and then end his day with Compline.*

A few weeks before their life changed completely, Sr. Silouani went for a drive with some friends. She took the red scarf she had around her neck and covered her hair with it so that the wind from the open window would not make a mess of it. "Perhaps you'll put on a head scarf for good someday," her friend teased. It was a joke, an offhand comment, and no one paid much attention to it. But sometimes prophecies come in the least expected ways.

A few days later, Sr. Silouani and her husband visited the monastery so they could speak with Gerontissa Philareti. "We just wanted to come to make sure that, since we have no children, if something happens to us, you will pray for us and do memorials* for us occasionally," they told her.

"Of course we will!" Gerontissa responded.

And then two weeks later, at the persistence of her husband, Sr. Silouani agreed that they would each go to a monastery for a few weeks as a trial. They did this with the blessing of their spiritual father in order to see if they would be willing to live out their days as monastics. Her husband went to the Holy Mountain, and at the advice of her spiritual father, she returned to Gerontissa Philareti's monastery.

After this trial period, they both returned home and went to visit their spiritual father. They spoke about their experiences and, although she was not as enthused as her husband initially, to his great surprise and delight Sr. Silouani said, "I will stay at the monastery."

It was decided. Their spiritual father told them, "Well then, this will be the last time you communicate, until you communicate in heaven." He did this because he knew it would make it easier for them both to focus on their respective monastic lives—as hard as it may seem to us from the outside.

Every now and again, Sr. Silouani would send some of her famous spinach-pitas to him through friends, and the men took great delight in watching her husband eat them to see if he recognized her special recipe.

Truly Sr. Silouani and her husband fulfilled Christ's admonition, "For there are eunuchs who were born thus from *their* mother's womb, and there are eunuchs who were made eunuchs by men, and there are eunuchs who have made themselves eunuchs for the kingdom of heaven's sake. He who is able to accept *it*, let him accept *it*" (Matt. 19:12).

Learning about Greece

IT WAS THE BEGINNING OF AUGUST, and we were fasting before the Feast of the Dormition of the Mother of God. I was to stay at the monastery until the feast day so I could practice my Greek. Living with my husband, both being native English speakers, we naturally didn't speak Greek to each other very often. So we both needed to spend time immersing ourselves in the language before we started our degrees at the university.

I stayed in one of the small guest rooms with just a bed, a table, and a closet. It had a very uneven floor and lots of icons on the walls. It was hot inside, but it was a sweet little room.

During my stay, since I was often the only pilgrim, they would set my food out on the little table and I would eat by myself. The nuns always ate lunch together in their own dining hall, accompanied by spiritual reading. This was their only opportunity to speak all together each day, go over some practical things, and for the abbess to instruct them on spiritual matters.

One particular day after lunch, once most of the nuns had left the kitchen, I went to make myself a coffee so that I could read for an hour or so in my room. (Every afternoon the sisterhood takes an hour break after lunch.) At this point I was close enough to the nuns that I helped myself. Sometimes I even made *them* coffee, which was a nice reversal for me. I liked being able to do something for them since they were always serving me.

As I made my coffee, Sr. Arsenia, one of the cooks, fried eggplant. She felt she had too much work to take a break. At the window, on a ladder, was Mr. John, one of the two regular workers from the nearby village. He was painting the outside windows while having a conversation with Sr. Arsenia.

"Mr. John, did you know that tomorrow we celebrate the Feast of the Transfiguration?" she asked.

"No, what's that?" he responded.

"It's one of the feasts of the Lord. Christ took His disciples, Ss. John, James, and Peter, with Him to the top of a mountain. You know St. John, right, the young man at the foot of the cross in icons?" she asked.

"Yes," he answered.

"On the mountaintop Christ was transfigured before them. His human body was illuminated by His divinity, revealing His true nature as both perfect God and perfect Man," she explained.

"Oh really, I didn't know that," he said with a gentle smile.

"That's why we'll eat fish tomorrow—for the feast," she added.

"Oh, okay. Well, I finished here; I'm going to move the ladder over. Have a good afternoon!" he said, descending.

As he climbed down, I walked over to Sr. Arsenia. "Did you just tell him about the Feast of the Transfiguration?" I asked.

"Yes."

"You mean he didn't know about it?"

"No, Constantina. Most people don't know much about the Church. He is faithful, but he just doesn't know a lot. He is a very good person. We try to tell him some things, but we have to be very careful," she answered.

"Why?" I asked, perplexed.

"Whatever we say to people, they may repeat to others. If we've said something wrong, then they will become scandalized because 'a nun said it'," she explained.

I was somewhat surprised by hearing this. I didn't know yet just how easy it is for people to become scandalized, nor did I know that most people in Greece have very high expectations of monastics. I would even venture to say *unreasonably* high expectations. After living in Greece a few more years, I began to see this for myself.

Here's an example. One afternoon Mrs. Maria (Sr. Silouani's sister) and I were sitting on a bench in the courtyard outside. She looked up and saw some spider webs in the eves. Pointing to them, she said to me: "The nuns need to clean those out before the patron saint's feast day."

I asked, "The spider webs? Why?"

"Because the women will see them and think the nuns never clean the monastery," she answered.

"Who cares? They're outside!"

"Yes, but some women go to other people's homes just to see how clean they're kept," she explained.

I was becoming more annoyed the more she explained. Just then Sr. Akakia walked by.

"Sister, you have to make sure you clean out those spider webs," Mrs. Maria told her.

Sr. Akakia looked in the direction Mrs. Maria's finger was pointing. "Yes, Mrs. Maria, but we don't have time right now. We have other things we need to clean."

I looked intently at Mrs. Maria. "You should tell those women they need to spend less time looking at how clean other people's homes are and more time looking at whether or not their *hearts* have spider webs in them!"

Mrs. Maria just laughed. She knew it was silly for people to care about outdoor spider webs, but unfortunately, people do.

The Ways of God

SR. EUPHEMIA AND I WERE preparing juice to bring to some of the nuns in the bakery. I confided to her that I found it odd that, after spending a significant amount of time with the nuns, I had never seen them get into a quarrel or even show outward signs of irritation—they were always very controlled in their responses. I asked her why this was, because in my experience of women, "squabbles" (as my mother would call them) were a frequent occurrence.

Personally, I've always found that it is a lot easier for women to fall into the habit of bickering than for men. The nuns, however, always displayed a willingness to help each other and a calm approach to the most stressful situations. As a result, the environment in the monastery always remained peaceful and pleasant.

This was Sr. Euphemia's response: "It's because if I notice a sister who seems particularly irritable and I think to myself, 'Gee, she's quite irate today,' I know that for certain tomorrow I will be the same way. If we judge someone, God allows us to fall into the same sin—to humble us," she answered. And I have to say that I cannot count how many times my own experience has verified what she said to me that day.

A few years later, Sr. Sarah, Sr. Thekla, and I were having a conversation, and this very topic came up. I mentioned this same thing to them, and Sr. Thekla explained it in this way:

"If someone were to come to a monastery and see the monastics arguing or being upset with one another, they would think to themselves, 'What's the point in coming here? This isn't a spiritual place.

They are no different from everyone else in the world.' They would be disheartened and receive no spiritual benefit from visiting the monastery.

"It's not that we don't get into quarrels or get upset with each other; it's just that God doesn't allow you to see it. He protects you and everyone else so you won't become scandalized.

"For example, once during a vigil of the Presanctified Liturgy,* Fr. Antonios, who often liturgizes here, became very weak from his strict fasting and nearly collapsed. He did not have a lot of strength by the end of the Liturgy, and he was afraid to commune the faithful because he feared, being weak, that he might spill the Holy Gifts.* So we put a big chair in front of the royal doors so he could commune the people sitting down. This could very easily scandalize someone.

"After the Liturgy was over, though, a woman who attended the service came up to me, and with tears in her eyes she said, 'That is the first time I've ever seen a priest commune people while kneeling down!'

"You see? She didn't even notice that he was sitting, not kneeling. From then on, though, Gerontissa told Fr. Antonios, 'Make sure you eat a good, hearty fasting meal the day you come to liturgize for us.'

"Another time we had the holy relics of the saints of the monastery out for veneration. That day I had just found out that my grandfather had died. While I was standing near the relics, I tried to control my emotions, but I was unable to, and so I was crying. A woman in the church saw me and said to Gerontissa with reverence, 'One of the sisters was so overcome with devotion to the saints that she was crying!' I wasn't crying out of devotion, but out of an emotional attachment to a family member. But God allowed her to be moved, thinking I was a good nun."

And when Sr. Thekla said "a good nun," she began to laugh, as though the idea that she would be considered a good nun was hilarious.

6

KNOT SIX

A Blessing from Gerontissa's Saint

IT WAS THE ABBESS'S NAME DAY,* and over a hundred pilgrims had come to visit her to wish her "many years" and "a good Paradise." Gerontissa, whose name is Philareti for a good reason, always laid out the red carpet for her guests. But on her name day she took it a step further.

The nuns had prepared a big meal for all the guests in the large dining hall. They set the two long tables on either side of the room with their best silverware and finest dishes. Napkins were carefully folded; everything was in order and the food was brought out. It always looked like a feast out of a medieval banquet—with the exception of meat. The sisters are well known for their talent in the kitchen, so the quality of the food matched the aesthetic of the beautifully laid-out dining hall.

After everyone ate, all those dishes were brought into the kitchen to be washed—twice. Yes, the nuns always wash everything twice! (This drove me crazy, personally. I know they were being careful to wash them all very well, but it always seemed so unnecessarily ascetical to me; I guess that's why they're nuns and I'm not.)

All of these dishes were then hand-dried. Among them were little fine glasses for wine, which were always handed to me with the warning, "Do not break this." Well, this is the glass Sr. Sarah was putting away in the cupboard when it slipped out of her hand and onto the floor. She cringed waiting to hear the sound of shattering glass. However, to everyone's utter amazement, it bounced! Once, twice, three times. It made the same sound the steel dishes used by monastics make when dropped: "ping, ping, ping." On the third bounce Sr. Sarah caught it.

Everyone stared wide-eyed. She crossed herself and with much gratitude said, "Thank you, St. Philaritos!"

Pray While You Work

THIS WONDERFUL HYMN to the Most Holy Theotokos is my personal favorite. It is also very popular in the monastery. A day has rarely passed while working with the nuns where I did not hear or join in saying the *Haritismous*, the Greetings, as the Greeks call this hymn. It's called "Greetings" because it consists of the various ways in which the Archangel Gabriel greeted our Lady Theotokos. It is written in Ancient Greek, which, contrary to what some may think, is not a language most Greeks understand. However, almost all the nuns have this memorized. Even Sr. Sarah has it memorized, and she is not a native speaker—no small feat! The nuns have a strong devotion to this divinely inspired hymn and say it every day, usually three times a day.

Sr. Xenia used to bring the hymn to elementary school with her as a child. While she should have been paying attention to her teacher, she would hide the little prayer book and memorize the hymn. Of course, it's easier to remember it in Greek because it is written in acrostic.* It was purposefully written this way to make it easier for the faithful to remember. Unfortunately, in translation this helpful key to memorization is lost.

The nuns pray this hymn so often because their spiritual father, a hermit from the Holy Mountain, praised its great influence. He once told them, "If even just one person on a plane or a train or in a car was praying the Akathist* hymn to the Mother of God and an accident was about to occur, it could save all those present." This is the power of the Mother of God's prayers.

Similarly, St. Cosmas the Aetolian tells a story about a thief whom the devil wanted to overthrow completely. The evil one was unable to, though, because the thief—who, as a child, had memorized and said the Akathist hymn daily to the Mother of God—had persisted in saying it each day, despite the fact that he lived an ungodly life. The practice of this prayer alone was enough to keep at bay his destruction by the devil, even while he lived a sinful life.

Eventually the devil's plot to kill him was revealed through the intercession of a holy Geronda.* This thief lived with a band of thieves in the mountains, and one day a holy Geronda happened to come upon their hideout. Spiritually perceiving something to be awry, the holy Geronda asked to see all those who lived there. They all came out, and being bound by Christ, the devil (in the guise of the cook) told the Geronda, "I have waited fourteen years to kill this man and take his soul to hell. But I have not found one day in which he has neglected to read the 'Archangel came' [the Akathist] prayer."[9]

On hearing the devil's plot, the thief repented and became a monk—as did some of his fellow-thieves. Oh, the power and protection the Mother of God grants to us, her unworthy children!

I was inspired when we prayed this hymn, and it encouraged me to memorize it in English, especially since many Greek faithful have it memorized. But unfortunately, I am ashamed to admit, I have not accomplished that yet.

This is the way they pray it in the monastery. One nun begins by saying, "An angel and the chiefest among them was sent from Heaven to cry, Rejoice, to the Theotokos," at which point another nun (and sometimes I, to my great delight) says in plain chant, "Most Holy Theotokos, save us!" This exchange is repeated three times.

Then the first nun continues, praying the first stanza. Each time the first nun says, "Rejoice, thou Bride Unwedded!" the second nun chants this same line after her. When the first nun says "Alleluia" at the end of each stanza, again the second nun chants "Alleluia" in response. At the end of the hymn, during the last stanza, again "Most Holy Theotokos, save us" is repeated three times in response to, "O All-hymned Mother who didst bear the Word and art more holy than all the saints." Once the Akathist hymn is finished, the "O Theotokos and Virgin, rejoice O Mary" is said three times. Although the hymn may seem long, it takes just over ten minutes to say it like this, because it is *said*, not sung—and Greeks have a tendency to say it quickly.

The Jesus Prayer and Humility

ALL THE NUNS HAVE THE ESSENTIAL HABIT of saying the Jesus Prayer* while working, while cleaning, while walking, and while eating.

They all say it very faintly and sometimes not audibly. It makes a real impact on the working environment. It serves as a constant reminder to talk less and pray more. In fact, this habit of praying while working became so engrained in me just by spending time with them that the Jesus Prayer is an automatic response when I begin to mop the floors in my own home.

I always found it helpful to be around so many people praying because as soon as my ears caught the slight whisper of the nuns' prayer, my wandering mind was called back to "Lord Jesus Christ, have mercy on me." It also helped to curb my loose tongue, because I knew the more I engaged them in conversation, the more I took them away from prayer.

One nun in particular said the Jesus Prayer so often that I do not remember ever once being in her presence and *not* hearing her pray. I liked to listen to her and pray along with her inside my mind. She would say, "Lord Jesus Christ, have mercy on me; Most Holy Theotokos, save us; through the prayers of the monastery founder, Lord Jesus Christ, have mercy on me; through the prayers of the monastery's patron, Lord Jesus Christ, have mercy on us." I really liked that she would not only say the Jesus Prayer, but combine intercession to the monastery's saints with her prayer. No doubt this was also a helpful tactic to keep her mind focused on the prayer.*

She was such a sweet, simple nun. It always made a huge impression on me that whenever I would ask her something, like what work I should do next, she would never tell me, but ask another nun. She was one of the older nuns, and yet she acted as if she were the youngest novice. She seemed to do all this without being conscious of it in any way.

This, it seemed to me, was true humility. I'll never forget her simple but perfect example. I only hope I come to imitate her.

A Higher Education

DURING A VISIT ONCE, a kind man dropped off a sack full of walnuts for the sisters. So Gerontissa asked me to shell all the walnuts in the sack so the sisters could cook with them. I used a hammer to open each shell; I took out the meat, put it in a bowl, and continued. Sr. Markella and Sr. Christodora were with me in the workroom just off the kitchen. Sr. Christodora was cleaning and chopping vegetables from the garden, and Sr. Markella was sorting beans.

They were both older nuns, and Sr. Markella was a great-schema nun. She never learned to read or write because she came from a poor family with many children, and at the age of twelve she needed to go to work. She had a paralyzed arm since childhood, and the last four years or so she was wheelchair-bound. She was a remarkable person; I learned a lot from her.

Sr. Christodora was a very small, skinny, joyful nun. She was the kind of person who, when she saw babies, would pinch their cheeks and speak in a very loud baby voice, and then playfully tap their faces before walking away. Come to think of it, this is a common practice among Greek yia-yias generally.

Since we were working together, Sr. Christodora thought it best for us to pray the Akathist hymn. She began by saying some preliminary prayers and wanted Sr. Markella to say the *Di'evhon** before she started the Akathist. Sr. Markella became a little timid and said, "Let the child [meaning me] say it."

Sr. Christodora, who was funny and simple, yelled, "Markella, say the Di'evhon!"

"No, just let the child say it, so she can learn," Sr. Markella responded.

"Markella! You're a great-schema nun! *You* should say it!" Sr. Christodora loudly responded.

"*Di'evhon ton agion pateron emon* . . . Through the prayers of our holy fathers," Sr. Markella finally said, and we continued with the Akathist hymn.

The real reason Sr. Markella didn't want to say the Di'evhon was that she was afraid she would make a mistake. Although she had so many prayers memorized, since she was illiterate she was embarrassed to say prayers in front of other people. She may never have learned how to read, but she surely learned how to pray!

7

KNOT SEVEN

Gutting Fish and Talking about Love

ONE FALL I WENT to the monastery in order to help the sisterhood sort their freshly harvested olives. But when I went into the kitchen to say hello, I was enthusiastically invited to help them gut and clean the forty kilos of fish that had just arrived.

After scaling and gutting the fish, we handed them on to the nuns in charge of washing them. Nothing is wasted in a monastery, so the heads remained intact. Of course I had only done this once before and was rather grossed out then, but every task was more pleasant when working alongside the nuns.

While scaling the fish with Sr. Marina, I told her how I had just read the Gospel passage in which Christ says, "By this all will know that you are My disciples, if you have love for one another" (John 13:35).

"I thought if people really wanted to see true Christian love, all they need to do is come to a monastery," I said.

"There are a lot of people in the world who have a lot of love too, Constantina," she said. "For example, we know this man who had written his dissertation when he was a student at university. One of his fellow students had somehow gotten hold of his paper and handed it in as his own. When this man found out, he was so angry he ran laps around the university, not knowing what else to do. He knew he had to forgive him, and after some time he was able to. Not only did he forgive him, he never revealed that his fellow student plagiarized his work. Is that not love?"

"Of course it is, Sister," I answered.

"And many people, whole Christian families, visit the sick and the suffering in hospitals. People in the world have a lot of love, not just in the monastery," she finished, and slightly tilting her head she sighed.

"I know, Sr. Marina. It's just that I think when someone who hasn't experienced a lot of love in the world comes to a monastery, the love shown to him can make a great impact."

SR. XENIA AND I had a similar conversation about love. We were mopping the floors in the bakery, and she started telling me a story she heard in a homily on almsgiving. The Geronda had said that almsgiving isn't just about giving money, but about loving our neighbor. So, to stress this point, he told a story about a man he met while giving a talk one day at a parish. This is how Sr. Xenia recounted the story to me:

"While the Geronda was speaking at the parish, he noticed a man with a perplexed look on his face, like he wanted to ask a question.

After speaking a while longer, he finally asked the man if something was bothering him. The man told him he had only come to the homily because a friend had asked him to and that he didn't believe the miraculous stories the Geronda had told about Christ. After further conversation in private, the Geronda managed to persuade the man to confess. All of this came about through his faithful friend, since it was at her prompting that the man decided to come at all.

"Time passed and the woman came to visit the Geronda. He was happy to have the opportunity to ask how her friend was. To his surprise, she told him that soon after they had met, the man fell ill. In fact, she had asked him to move in with her in order to take care of him. He ended up in the hospital. Fearing that he was going to die, she called for a priest so that he could receive Holy Communion before departing from this life. Unfortunately, by the time the priest arrived, the man had fallen into a coma and was unresponsive. With tears in her eyes, the woman got down on her knees and began praying for him to wake up. Just then the man sat up, communed of the Holy Mysteries and said, "'My Lord, take me now that I have You inside of me, that I may not be separated from You!'

"He lay back down and peacefully fell asleep in the Lord," Sr. Xenia finished. Wiping tears away from her cheeks, she said, "Ah, people in the world have so much love! The Geronda finished his homily by saying that what that woman did for her friend was the greatest almsgiving one can do—she saved a soul by bringing him to confession and helping him receive Holy Communion. God won't ask her for much more than that!"

So, it turns out whether you are in the world or in a monastery, you can learn both to love and to see love around you.

KNOT SEVEN

Monastic Cares

A WEEK BEFORE THE MONASTERY'S feast day, my husband and I went out to help the sisterhood prepare. On their feast day they receive almost two thousand people, to whom they offer a simple meal of *fasolada*, bean soup, cooked on an open fire. The monastery has kept this tradition for at least five centuries.

In earlier years, hundreds of locals from surrounding villages would come to the monastery on foot. Starting out early the day before, they made sure they arrived in time for the festival Liturgy. Needless to say, a lot of work goes into pulling off their feast day, and so they get a lot of help from friends and family.

My husband and I went early to help organize, package, and label their various sweets, soaps, and tea. Of course, apart from this, we also helped in the general cleaning of the monastery. As the days passed and we approached the feast day, the dishes in the kitchen piled up (even higher than they usually do). Since so many people came to help, the nuns had about fifty extra settings for each meal to deal with.

One afternoon I woke up about fifteen minutes later than I had wanted to from siesta. I hastily made my bed and ran for the kitchen. To my surprise, no one was there yet. As I was looking at all those dishes, a wave of anxiety came over me.

Oh no! The sisters slept in and I don't have any way of waking them up! How are we ever going to get all these dishes washed, dried, and put away in time to make supper and then clean those dishes?! They're going to be here all night! I thought to myself.

Then Sr. Euphemia came into the kitchen, walking slowly and looking sleepy.

"Sister, I woke up late and ran to get here. I had so much anxiety looking at all these dishes and I didn't know how I would wake you up!"

Just then Sr. Hara came in eating a piece of cake. Sr. Theologia, dragging her feet, came in after her and sat on a chair near the door.

"Sisters, I didn't know where you were, and I was just standing here looking around and looking at the clock, wondering how in the world we're ever going to get these dishes done!"

They greeted my display of anxiety with broad smiles. "We know we'll be here until well after midnight, so we didn't rush to get in," Sr. Theologia said.

"You have what we call 'monastic cares,' Constantina," Sr. Euphemia said.

Turning towards Sr. Theologia, she said, "She's worrying about getting her *diakonema** done before the day is over!

"Here you are having an anxiety attack about the work you feel you need to do, while we stagger in with Sr. Hara eating cake!" she said, patting my back.

At this we all laughed.

It's nice to know that although the nuns struggle with their own anxieties at times, they are able to take all the work they have to do in stride. I can't go there without seeing the work I did that day in my sleep, whether it's sorting olives or stocking the bookstore. They just laugh: "You have monastic cares," they tease. They give it a nice name; I just call it plain old anxiety.

The Power of Prayer

SR. SARAH SHARED WITH ME an impressive story about the power of prayer. Sr. Agapia's sister and brother-in-law came to visit her at the monastery, and her brother-in-law told her:

"Agapia, I saw your father in a dream. He was in a dark place but was not distressed. He told me he was happy there because whenever you pray for him, a light brightens his darkness, and the day you were tonsured a nun he was surrounded by light!"

I have read similar incredible stories in different books. An oral tradition claims as many as seven generations in a monastic's family can be benefited from his or her tonsure, as many as fourteen generations in the family of a priest. "That is, provided the priest is a *good* priest," Gerontissa would tell us. It seems to me that this is God's way of finding any excuse He can to grant His mercy and love to us sinners.

Let Us, O Faithful, Welcome Christ's Transfiguration

IT WAS THE FEAST of the Transfiguration of Christ, and although I was exhausted, I slowly made my way from the guest house to the church for the vigil. As usual, the lights were off, the oil lamps lit, and the candle boxes full of candles—the smoke of which rose up as a symbolic prayer for the numerous souls and causes they burned for.

I entered the nave and venerated the icon of Christ's Transfiguration that lay on the white embroidered covering of the icon stand. Beside it was a large candle stand that had a wooden portion near the top with intricately painted flowers and vines in pink, blue, purple, and green. The large beeswax candle burning above it illumined the white-clothed figure of Christ; it illumined the shining light surrounding Him and the figures of the apostles, who, stunned by the vision, were lying prostrate. Christ was revealing Himself as the perfect Radiance of the Father, the pre-eternal Word, begotten of the Father before all ages.

Shine Your light also on me, your lowly servant, I whispered as I kissed His feet.

I made my way to a stasidi on the left side of the church—the designated section for women—standing in the one closest to the icon of the patron saint. I examined all the silver and gold rectangular plaques lined up on the bottom of his icon, each one embossed with a different body part: arms, eyes, legs, and hearts. They are called *tamata*, and many faithful buy them and place them on miracle-working icons in supplication for health or healing of the particular body part depicted.

I was tired and not particularly in the mood for a vigil after a day of work. It was still the beginning of Matins when I told myself, *It's one of the Great Feasts, wake up and pay attention!*

Yet I couldn't rouse myself or inspire myself to feel moved by such a wonderful feast.

I wonder how long this is going to take . . . My mind wandered again.

Shut up and say the prayer! I fought back.

Time passed, I struggled not to fall asleep, and especially not to fall over during those few moments I did fall asleep while standing on my feet. I made sure to always have one hand holding the stasidi, just in case.

"*Doxa see to theexadi to fos…* Glory to Thee who hast shown us the light," the nuns chanted.

Okay, really, wake up now. The Liturgy is about to start, I told myself.

I shook myself awake, just in time to see Sr. Akakia and Sr. Arsenia moving from lighting the candles in the chandelier to lighting the candles on the corona—the larger, circular chandelier that encircles the main chandelier (most often found in monastery churches).

They each held a long wooden rod with a small flame on the end. Facing each other, they began to light each individual candle in the large, golden corona. And before I knew it the whole nave was encompassed in light.

Having lit all the candles on her side, Sr. Arsenia walked back to the narthex, with her black ecclesiarch's robe flowing behind her.

Returning, she handed Sr. Akakia a different long, wooden rod with a metal hook on the end. Standing on opposite sides once again, they each placed a rod on one side of the corona. Slowly and carefully they pushed the rods in opposite directions, causing the corona to sway, turning left and right, the icons of the apostles and patriarchs now moving in rhythm.

Before exiting this time, Sr. Arsenia reached up and gently held the golden right hand of blessing that points downward, attached to the bottom of the chandelier. Ever so slightly she turned it, causing the large chandelier to also sway in a circular motion.

I was taken aback. I had only seen this once, during Pascha at a monastery in America. I didn't know they did this for other liturgical feasts.

As soon as the chandelier began swaying, I noticed Sr. Akakia in front of the icon of Christ in the iconostasis. As Sr. Arsenia had done to the hand of blessing, she too gently held the bottom of the large, silver oil lamp and guided it to sway in a circle. Next, she approached the icon of the Mother of God. Bowing and crossing herself, she kissed her before putting to motion her oil lamp. I stepped back, allowing Sr. Akakia more room as she approached the icon of the patron saint. His icon was lit by three oil lamps. She spun the one in the middle first, the other two afterward.

As the nuns began chanting the troparion* for the feast, the whole nave was basking not only in light, but in moving light.

"*Metamorfotheis en to orei Hriste o Theos* . . . O Thou who wast transfigured upon the mountain, Christ our God, and shewedst to Thy disciples Thy glory, as they were able to bear it: kindle Thine everlasting light even upon us sinners, by the prayers of the Mother of God. O Giver of Light, glory be to Thee!"

The cosmos was swaying in glorious anticipation of the celebration of Christ's revelation to the world as perfect God and perfect Man. And what had I been doing in anticipation?

O Lord, I was found sleeping when I should have been watching. Enlighten me with Your everlasting light, as far as I can bear it, and forgive me, a sinner.

Reflecting thus, I bowed low and made the sign of the cross as the priest intoned, "Blessed is the Kingdom of the Father, and of the Son, and of the Holy Spirit."

KNOT EIGHT

Magnify, O My Soul, the Mother of God

EVERY EVENING DURING THE TWO-WEEK fast period in preparation for the Feast of the Dormition of the Mother of God, the sisterhood prays the Supplication service to her. After the regular Vespers, they immediately begin the Supplicatory Canon.

I cherished those days, attending these services. The service—sung in the original Ancient Greek—flows so beautifully that one is moved regardless of whether or not he understands the words. Spiritually his heart understands and receives nourishment, for not only were the hymns divinely inspired, but the melodies of Byzantine chant are as well, as my chanting teacher used to say.

Since the nave was packed, I stood in front of the reliquary in the narthex with the icon of the Savior above it and listened attentively to the nuns' paradoxically passionless and emotion-filled voices.

Diaaaasosooooon . . . It was the way they stressed this particular word, which means "deliver" or "save us." They said it with such meaning, such pure emotion. I was moved by the inflection of their voices—the raw human voice crying out in supplication for the Mother of God to deliver us from danger. No foreign instrument accompanied them, only the melody carried by the *ison*,* in a low unobtrusive way.

The fact that I didn't know what *diasoson* meant didn't change my reaction. My heart understood they were pleading with the Mother of God solely from the intonation of their voices. This was so utterly powerful that it captivated my full attention each and every day I heard it, and each and every time my heart impulsively cried out with their voices for the Mother of God to attend to me. This is the power of Byzantine chant: "It inspires you; gives you strength. It elevates your soul to worship the Lord with all your attention," Sr. Raphaela said to me once when we were speaking about it.

Byzantine music was written so that the chanter can inflect the appropriate words to make a stronger impact. A good example of this that I can offer is St. Cassiane's hymn of the sinful woman, sung on Holy Tuesday.

The chanter at our parish church in Thessaloniki would chant this whole hymn very slowly and beautifully. (It took him eighteen minutes to chant it.) At the word *dexai*—which means "accept" or "receive"—he enunciated very loudly and from the bottom of his diaphragm. It made such an impact on the faithful that there was hardly a dry eye in the church after he reached the end of the hymn.

The purpose of this is not to evoke emotion in the listener—or even to impress—but to convey with music how the soul cries out to God. St. Cassiane describes a sinful woman: Having heard where the Son of the Virgin was staying, she ran to purchase costly ointment. Out of repentance she anointed Christ's feet, actively ridding herself of her sinful ways. And while she kissed and washed His feet, drying them with her unbound hair, she cried out, "*Accept* the fountain of my tears!" By stressing the first word of that phrase, the chanter communicates the forcefulness with which the sinful woman was repenting.

This is what the nuns communicated when they sang "deliver us." They chanted it in such a way that it conveyed the desperation and longing with which the soul cries out to the Mother of God, the saints, and the Lord to deliver it from all temptation, danger, passion, and sin.

Just as the sisters were finishing the Supplication service, while the Di'evhon was being said, they would turn off the lamp at the chanter's stand and turn toward the iconostasis. Before hymn books were in plenty, one chanter would say the verse so that the others knew what needed to be chanted. In keeping with this custom, Sr. Euphemia intoned the first line.

In plain chant she said, "*Epithimo Panagia mou* . . . I long very much, my Panagia* . . ." And in the sweetest, softest voices the nuns repeated the line according to the tone, "*Epithimo Panagia mou,*" in response. They continued this way until the end of the hymn, with Sr. Euphemia first saying the line in plain chant while the nuns' voices would overlap hers in repetition.

This particular hymn is not well known. It is from the Holy Mountain—the "Garden of the Panagia," as it is referred to in Greece. It is not in any hymnal that I have ever heard of, and the nuns chant it from memory. The author is unknown. The melody, Plagal of the Fourth Tone, Ode 3, is a familiar one:

I long very much, my Panagia
For the beauty of Paradise,

For the scent,
And the flowers,
And the sweetest fragrance
And the songs of the angels
When they sing to thy Son.

It was a beautiful way to finish the Supplication service and a wonderful way to praise our Lady Theotokos, the Queen of Heaven. May we find favor with her!

Cancer Martyrs

ONE AFTERNOON, SR. XENIA AND I were preparing jars for the jam and pickled vegetables the sisters make. While we were stacking the jars in crates to take to the bakery, a man from the village came in to speak with one of the nuns.

After he left, Sr. Xenia said to me, "Constantina, did you see that young man? He was married to a young woman, but she died of cancer when she was only twenty-nine years old. They hadn't been married for very long when she was diagnosed. She was a good Christian and never complained or asked why she had to have cancer. She accepted God's will.

"One night he saw her in his sleep. She was in a magnificent place with palaces and large houses. Seeing her there, he asked her, 'How are you? Where do you live?'

"'I live here and I am very happy,' she said.

"'What is this place?' he asked.

"'It's the place God has prepared for those martyred by cancer.

He allowed me to come here because I never asked Him, "Why me?" when I was ill, but accepted His will,' she answered.

"'How can *I* come to live here?' he asked.

"'You need to sell a lot of our things and give alms to the poor in my name,' she instructed him."

Looking at me as she finished, Sr. Xenia smiled, impressed by the story she had just told me.

"Man, the miracles that happen in everyday Orthodox life," I said. *What god is as great as our God?* I thought to myself.

Great-Schema Nun Markella

IF YOU HAD MET SR. MARKELLA when I did, you would notice that regardless of whether or not she has a prayer rope in her hand, her fingers make the motion as though she is pulling along her *komboskini.**

She would greet you with a large smile and sparkling eyes. She would ask you how you are, how your husband is, and how many children you have. If you told her you had none, she would tell you not to worry—that God would give them to you. If you look like me, she would tell you, "You have a body for having children. You are wide. This way the baby will have lots of room to move around!" She would say this while wiggling in her wheelchair trying to illustrate to you how a baby would have lots of room to "dance"—as she called it—in your womb. She would make you laugh with her unintentionally probing, yet adorable, questions and comments. You would quickly realize her joy is contagious.

The first few times I met her, I was blown away by her joy. She had so many health problems; the nuns had to take complete care of her. She was no longer able to walk, or even to stand. She had not had full use of her right arm since she was twelve years old.

Yet she always greeted you with a smile and would tell you to come close so she could kiss you on your cheeks. You would bend low each time and snatch a kiss from her hand—a blessing—knowing the kiss to be secured, since she can't pull her hand back from you.

She would again ask about your husband and tell you what a good boy he is, because she loves boys and they can do no wrong in her sweet (Greek) mindset. When you jokingly tell her, "He's fine, I'm the bad one," she would quickly agree with you and say, "He's an angel."

She would ask you to sit with her to "make company" and, if you knew her well, she would tell you some of the spiritual things she experiences.

You would listen in amazement, all the while knowing that she has no idea that she is betraying her spiritual height. Out of perfect humility and natural simplicity, she never thought for a moment that the things she tells you reveal, not only the miraculous ways of God, but her own worthiness of the gifts.

She may even ask you to get a tissue out of her pocket to clean her glasses or walk across the room to get her some water and then tell you how exactly she would like the water thermos placed on the shelf. You would see that she does all of this without a shade of shame; she is not embarrassed that she requires help and she does not hesitate to ask for it. She accepts her trials in the true spirit of humility. She does not have the egotism that is present in us who cannot accept help from others; we who are ashamed to ask for help, or accept it when it is offered.

It seems to me, recognizing that we need help and being able to accept it when it's offered is the first step to acquiring humble-mindedness.

If we can't receive the help of our neighbor, whom we see, how will we be able to trust and accept the help of God, whom we do not see?

Sr. Markella saw and received help offered, and asked for it when it was necessary. She didn't mind disturbing you, and you didn't mind going out of your way to help her, since you had come to learn from her example. In one way or another we are always dependent—be it on a parent, on a friend, a spouse, and *always* on God. Joyfully and graciously receiving help is a true sign of spiritual maturity, and Sr. Markella had mastered that.

KNOT NINE

An Open Grave and a Monastic Mindset toward Death

ONCE AGAIN, DURING A VISIT leading up to the monastery's feast day, John and I were helping the nuns clean the monastery's museum. It displays some of the old tools used in the monastery throughout the many years of its existence. The collection includes tools for harvesting olives, an olive press, *prosphora** seals, large wooden bread trays used in old stone ovens, and so forth. While John and I were dusting the different tools, Sr. Theologia was climbing a ladder to clean one of the windows. At some point the ladder became unsteady, and it startled her.

"It'll help you fear death," I said playfully.

"Constantina, we shouldn't fear *death*," she said. "We should fear the furnace [hell]. Many people mistakenly fear death, though," she added and continued working.

A little while later, she said, "Did you know we had the workers open some graves for us in the graveyard? Yia-yia and Sr. Markella are getting older and we want to be ready."

"Yeah, someone mentioned that to us," I said.

"Well, we went to the graveyard to see the graves, and Sr. Seraphima wanted to make sure it was big enough for her because she's really tall. So she got into one and lay down. When the workers saw her, they got upset and started shouting, 'Get out of there, what are doing?'

"We asked them, 'You know we might die before the yia-yias do, don't you?'

"Mr. Theodore said, 'No, don't say such a thing! You're young; don't think that way!'

"The workers were upset and frightened at the thought that we believed it possible for us to die before the yia-yias. Many Greeks are like that. They fear death a lot," she explained. "They think of it in a superstitious way, as though talking about death or getting into a grave will somehow cause death to come sooner," Sr. Theologia finished.

"That's sad," John commented.

Something I Heard Confirmed by Experience

I HEARD A HOMILY by the Cypriot priest-monk, Archimandrite Zacharias of Essex, in which he says there are two ways to acquire humility: either by condemning yourself or by acquiring complete gratitude toward God. He claims these two seemingly opposite paths both lead to humble-mindedness. Although I believed and accepted that gratitude toward God for all things was a wonderful virtue, I could not see the two different approaches as equal. I couldn't quite accept that humble thoughts could be attained without crying for one's sins or internally condemning oneself. The following conversation changed my perspective.

One evening I accompanied one of the nuns outside the monastery to where the garbage bins were located. We were speaking about hypothyroid and I mentioned that I am supposed to get periodic tests done for this because something was discovered in a blood test once upon a time that revealed I would develop this condition.

The sister said, "A few of the nuns have it, and it causes their emotions to be a bit off. They cry easily."

"Well, that's good then," I said smiling. "They can use it for ammunition to have tears for their sins!"

"It's not necessary to always think of yourself as a sinner. Sometimes it's better to be grateful to God, and if you make mistakes to accept your fall, rise again, and ask God for forgiveness," she responded.

I stubbornly tried to explain how I saw it in a different way and thought the "hard path"—as Elder Porphyrios of Athens calls it—was the better path.

She disagreed with me: "We also should remember that we are made in the image of God and that He is merciful and does not desire the death of a sinner, but rather that the sinner should turn and live."

The conversation continued for quite some time, and I left it rather baffled because I did not feel as though we had come to a common conclusion. I even felt as though we were speaking past each other.

All of this sat with me for some days until one evening, when we were mopping the floors in the bookstore, this sister started to open up to me. In order to help me, she told me some things about herself and her past that revealed her character a bit more. She had had a troubled background—one filled with sadness and difficulties.

"I don't have a blessing to think too much about hell or the Judgment," she told me, smiling in a way that revealed a low opinion of herself.

Hearing this, I realized that the "hard path" really is not for everyone—especially those prone to despondency or despair. And it is not necessarily better; it's just a different path to reliance on God and not on self. The words of Elder Joseph the Hesychast* came to mind then. In speaking about the different characters of people, he said, "First of all, my child, know that there are great differences from man to man and monk to monk. There are souls with a soft character that are very easily persuaded. There are also souls with a tough character that are not subordinated so easily. They are as different as cotton is from iron. Cotton needs only to be rubbed with words, but iron requires fire and a furnace of temptations to be worked."[10]

Those that need to "do violence" (Matt. 11:12) to themselves should condemn themselves in their thoughts and struggle to overcome their sins with tears, pleading for God to forgive them. For those who are naturally more sensitive, and especially those that struggle with certain forms of depression, they should try to mold their thoughts into a constant flowing stream of gratitude toward Christ and His mercy, His love, and His forbearance.

This second kind of person should avoid focusing on his or her sins too much, so that he or she does not despair. We all need to see our sins, mistakes, and passions and confess them, feel sorry for them, but ultimately struggle with more resolve not to continue in them.

What I couldn't grasp from hearing, I learned from experience. Some characters are different. What I think is right for me is not right for everyone.

An Invisible Monk

SR. THEKLA'S YOUNG COUSINS were visiting the monastery once, and she had taken them for a walk around the monastery. On returning to the guesthouse, as they were walking by the fountain in the center of the courtyard, one of the children suddenly exclaimed, "There's a *papouli** over there!"

"Where?" Sr. Thekla asked.

"Over there near the fountain," the child answered.

"Well, go and get his blessing then!" Sr. Thekla told them.

The children walked toward the fountain, and the little boy sort of bowed his head while leaning forward and kissed what seemed to be the air. Sr. Thekla took the children back into the guesthouse and asked them, "What did the papouli look like? What color hair did he have?" thinking perhaps they had seen a saint. She started showing the children different icons and photos of well-known saints and elders. When they noticed a framed photograph of the monastery's spiritual father on the wall, the children said, "That's him! That's who we saw."

Yia-yia Paraskevi revealed a similar experience once. One of the sisters was attending to Yia-yia and asked her off-handedly if she felt sad that the sisterhood saw their spiritual father a lot less frequently than they used to. Over a decade prior, he left the cenobitic monastery he lived in on the Holy Mountain to stay in the desert as a hermit. And so his visits to the monastery became fewer and contact with him became more infrequent. To the nun's surprise, Yia-yia answered, "I see him every day; every day he is in our church praying for us at the altar, commemorating us during the Divine Liturgy."

A faithful woman from Athens whom my husband and I became very close to told us the following story: Once, she decided in the middle of the night to take a train up to the village where the monastery is located in order to visit the sisters for a few days. She told us that around one-thirty AM she suddenly had the idea to leave that morning for the monastery. So she slept a few hours and at five AM, full of joy at the prospect of visiting her favorite monastery, she was off in a taxi to the train station.

"I had only traveled by myself once before, but this time I felt like I was with really good company. I was so joyful on the train! It didn't feel at all like I was traveling alone."

She arrived at the monastery and enjoyed her pilgrimage there, as she always had. A few days later she returned to Athens by train and took a taxi home that evening.

"Just as I put my key in the door, suddenly I felt as though someone had left me; I was alone again. So that evening I called my spiritual father and I said, 'Geronda, you're going to laugh at me if I tell you what I'm thinking!'"

Narrating this to us, she turned red and began to giggle nervously, probably just the way she did while speaking to her spiritual father: "'You're going to think I'm crazy, Geronda.' I told him.

"'Tell me,' my spiritual father said, also laughing.

"'Even though I was all alone, I felt as though I had traveled to the monastery with company. Only just now on placing my key in the keyhole did I feel as though I was alone again.'

"'That's right, my child, because the spiritual father of the monastery was with you.'

"'What, Geronda?' I asked him.

"'He traveled to the monastery with you, and on your return home he left you,' he explained to me."

Accepting what she heard from her spiritual father—who was

himself a well-loved spiritual father—she was humbled that a great hermit such as the monastery's spiritual father would accompany her, if invisibly.

Afterward she became embarrassed for having told us this story because she did not want it to seem as though she felt herself worthy of such an experience—and it was clear she did not. But we assured her it only testified to the spiritual height of the monastery's spiritual father and not hers. (Of course, it *does* testify to her state of spirituality, but to protect her from the soul-destroying sin of pride, we told her it didn't.)

During one of the occasions when the sisterhood's spiritual father came to visit the sisters—visibly this time!—they laid aside all their scheduled work in order to listen to him. Every day they prepared the meals, but left the dishes unwashed so they had more time to listen to his instruction about the spiritual life. Meals went by, days went by, and the dishes continued to pile up, while the sisters soaked up all the things their elder had to tell them. They made confession and listened to his God-inspired words.

A few guests who had come to speak with the elder were staying at the monastery, and seeing all those dishes, they knew what work lay ahead for the sisterhood. One night, while these women were sleeping in the guest rooms, one of them awoke, and glancing out the window, she saw that the lights were on in the kitchen.

She woke up the woman who was staying with her to tell her, "I bet those nuns are doing the dishes in the middle of the night! We'd better go help them." They walked through the passageway that led to the kitchen. Their suspicions were confirmed: they could hear running water and clinking dishes. The door, however, was locked. So they walked outside and tried the other door to the kitchen, but that too was locked.

"Forget it, then!" one of the women said, and they both went back to bed.

The next day all the dishes were washed, dried, and put away. But the nuns were as surprised as the pilgrims to find everything in order. They hadn't done it, and they didn't know who did! Was it perhaps a little help sent from God through the prayers of their elder?

10

KNOT TEN

If These Should Keep Silent, the Stones Will Cry Out

DURING AN UNFORTUNATE FEW YEARS, before the current abbess came to restore the monastery, the community had declined until only one nun remained. Shepherds and various villagers came and took over the monastery for their own uses. Monastic life had come to a standstill, and the once beautiful and flourishing community was no more. (Much of this was due to pillaging, occupation, and murder perpetrated by some Muslims from a neighboring country.)

Many historically and spiritually valuable things were stolen, including old and revered icons, and the general state of the monastery was poor due to many years of neglect. During those regrettable days, the six-hundred-year-old cross with the crucified Christ located on the altar in the sanctuary was among the holy objects that were stolen. Many years later, once Gerontissa Philareti and the nuns came to occupy and restore the monastery, God saw fit for this icon to be found and returned.

It was late November when Sr. Theologia enthusiastically told me the news: One of the stolen icons had been found in Europe. The icon was a fourteenth-century Byzantine altar cross, intricately painted in the traditional Byzantine style. Apparently a wealthy Greek shipowner who lived in Spain had died, and his son was trying to sell this cross from his father's collection.

It was offered to a gallery in the United Kingdom, but the UK, checking the list of stolen artifacts, noticed it was listed as stolen. The gallery notified Scotland Yard, and they were able to track down the owner's family, which ultimately led to charges being brought. All of this was due to the Providence of God, of course.

The monastery had been informed that the cross had been found, and a vague pledge was made to return it by Christmas, but first it would visit various Greek museums. The sisterhood anxiously anticipated the icon's arrival. However, the fast for the Nativity came and went. The Nativity feast, then Epiphany came and went. Weeks leading up to Great Lent, the Triodion season, and most of Great Lent passed, and still there was no sign of the Byzantine altar cross.

All of this was the plan of God, it seems; for no one could have anticipated that the Lord would choose to return the icon to the monastery on Palm Sunday, such an appropriate day for its arrival. The nuns had the monastery looking its finest with ribbons and flowerpots, banners and flags hung up everywhere. Government officials, hierarchs, clergy, laity, and even the military were all there to greet the Lord on His entrance into the monastery.

As the car carrying the cross was winding down the hill, the soldiers stood at attention and everyone watched with expectant eyes. Four soldiers, two of whom were relatives of one of the sisters, hoisted the funeral bier used on Holy Friday on their shoulders. They were to carry Christ from the parking lot through the courtyard and into the church. He came into Jerusalem on a humble donkey on Palm Sunday and entered the monastery on the same day with great honor more than two thousand years later.

The Byzantine cross was placed on the bier, and the soldiers entered the monastery's courtyard. The nuns were lined up across the courtyard from the main gate to the church with palms in their hands while the bells rang out announcing His arrival. Who but the King of Kings and Lord of Lords could have orchestrated a better day for the cross to return to the monastery, to take its place on the altar?

It's All Greek to Me!

ON ONE OF MY FIRST VISITS to the monastery, I was asked to help Sr. Philothei and Sr. Arsenia make cheese pies. I still hadn't learned the Greek language well and did not yet know that Sr. Arsenia knew English. Many times the nuns would not speak English to me, so I would end up being surprised when I couldn't understand something and they would explain it in English.

I was helping the sisters get the ingredients ready, but before we started I thought I should go to the washroom. I knew that Greeks often say, "I am going to the toilet," but it seemed rather uncouth to me to say "toilet"; I preferred to say *banio* (washroom).

But I didn't say, "I will go to the banio," because I thought when using the word *banio* in Greek the appropriate sentence was, "I will make banio."

You see, this *is* an appropriate Greek phrase; it's just when Greeks say it they don't mean, "I will use the washroom," as I thought.

So, when I said to the nuns, "I will help with the cheese-pies, but first I will make banio," I was surprised when they responded with giggles.

I looked perplexed, and they corrected me: "You mean you will go to the toilet."

"Yes," I said, thinking they were correcting me so that I would speak more naturally.

When I came back, Sr. Arsenia, who is a real tormentor, said to me in English, "And how was your bath, do you feel refreshed?"

And that is how I learned that to say, "I will make banio," means "I will bathe or shower," while to say, "I will *go* to the banio," means "I will go to the washroom," but Greeks don't say that very often.

After this I stopped thinking saying "toilet" was so boorish.

The Devil's Hatred

SR. SARAH AND I WERE in the storage room loading up crates of products to restock the bookstore. We had a list of how many jars of honey we needed and how many apricot, orange, and strawberry jams. We also took out half a crate worth of jars containing pickled vegetables, sauces, and sweets with a spoon (a Greek fruit dessert made with lots of syrup).

We went through the shelves of books and grabbed some more books by Elder Paisios of the Holy Mountain, as well as some of the practical books about dealing with depression and children born with Down Syndrome. We opened up the metal storage unit and searched for an icon of St. Christopher, a few more of St. John the Baptist, and a couple of the Great Feasts.*

While working we spoke about the fact that different people with different problems and backgrounds do not warrant one sweeping approach when it comes to speaking about the Orthodox faith. Since we both had experiences of people asking for and needing help, we were discussing the best ways to speak to people "where they're at."

We were discussing how sometimes it's easy to forget that prudence is necessary so that people do not feel offended by an approach that seems overly harsh (or "Greek," as we would sometimes jokingly call it, since Greeks are known for being rather blunt at times).

"Remind me to tell you a story when we're finished here," Sr. Sarah said.

We packed everything up and each took up a handle on the crate to carry it together. We made a few trips this way until we had everything ready to be put away in the bookstore.

It was late in the evening, the gate to the monastery was already closed, and there were no visitors. We put everything away, finished tidying up, swept and vacuumed.

"Here, sit down." Sr. Sarah gestured to a small wooden stool. She sat down beside me on another stool.

"Awhile back a young man from Western Europe had come to visit the monastery because he was hiking on a nearby trail in the mountains," she began telling me.

"He started speaking with me in the bookstore. He mentioned he was into Buddhism and was even speaking about some experiences he'd had. I had also experimented with Buddhism when I was younger. At that time in my life I was reaching out for some kind of spirituality but, by the grace of God, I didn't stay there and eventually found Orthodoxy. So when this young man started talking about Eastern religions, I became very concerned for him, knowing how dangerous that stuff can be."

At this point Sr. Sarah paused, sighed, and made her cross: "The devil hears everything we say!"

But she continued, "I started talking to him about the book, *Christ the Eternal Tao* by Hieromonk Damascene, and other things. I even told him some personal things about my own past (which a nun should rarely do) and at some point, without even realizing it, I began to say things that, although I understood what I was saying, I felt as though someone else was speaking with my voice. In fact I had not even previously known some of the things I was saying.

"I thought to myself, *I didn't even know that, how did I just say that?*

"After the conversation was over, he seemed to see things differently and even thought he'd look up that book I had mentioned. That evening I returned to my cell* and made the sign of the cross, perplexed as to what happened during that conversation. The next morning I woke up and could barely get out of bed.

"I was very stiff and sore and moved around with a lot of difficulty. I felt like I had been run over by a truck! I became very frightened, thinking back to the evening before, when I spoke with words that were not my own. So I ran to Sr. Paisia's cell."

Here I must explain that Sr. Paisia is Gerontissa Philareti's "right hand," as we say, and helps a lot of young people herself. She became a nun at the age of twelve. This sort of thing is of course unheard of in North America but very much a part of our Orthodox tradition. Her father had died and her mother had children to raise on her own, so she gave her daughter permission to fulfill her desire to become a monastic. Years later, Sr. Paisia's mother came to the monastery herself to join her daughter in the monastic life.

Sr. Paisia later became a great-schema nun, and many young couples came to the monastery to speak with her. She even kept her telephone on all night long so that people suffering from psychosis or demon possession, or any kind of trouble or temptation, could call her and find advice and comfort in her words.

Sr. Sarah continued, "I knocked on Sr. Paisia's cell door and said the Di'evhon. When she invited me in, I told her I needed to confess something I was worried about. I told her how sore I was when I woke up and that I feared it had something to do with the fact that while I spoke with the young man the evening before I started saying things I didn't even know myself. I also confessed that I had told the young man things about my own past.

"'No, you did the right thing. It was from the Holy Spirit,' she told me. 'You helped that young man, and you should speak as much as you can about those things to people so that you can help them. The devil was angry with you because of what you did, and that is why you felt so sore when you woke up this morning. Don't worry, you did the right thing!' she assured me. I was relieved to hear her say that," Sr. Sarah said.

We can never have enough examples of the evil one's malice to remind us that we do not do battle with mere flesh and blood, but "against principalities, against powers, against the rulers of the darkness of this age, against spiritual *hosts* of wickedness in the heavenly *places*" (Eph. 6:12).

KNOT ELEVEN

The Piercing Eyes and Soft Hands of a Saint

TO RETURN TO ELDER EVSEVIOS'S evening visit to the monastery: Once he arrived, Gerontissa sat with him for some time alone in the reception room. After she had a chance to speak with him in private, she invited the sisterhood and me to join them. I was very nervous. We all lined up to go into the room and take his blessing.

Whenever monastics line up, they go in order of oldest to youngest, not according to age, but according to how many years they have lived in the monastery. And so I lined up last, behind Sr. Thekla, because I was a layperson. In fact, other than the two men who came with the elder, I was the only layperson at the monastery that evening.

When we walked into the room, the elder was sitting on a chair in the center. His crutches were leaning against the wall. I will never forget how peaceful he looked. His hair and beard were completely white and he was wearing a tight knit woolen hat, the same kind Elder Paisios of the Holy Mountain is often seen wearing in photographs. He looked to be slouching and his head was bowed low and to the left a little, reminiscent of St. John Maximovitch in some photos.

Once I got past the entrance, his eyes turned towards me. I wasn't sure why he was staring at me, but I figured it was because I was a foreigner—not to mention the only laywoman there that night—and so I stood out. His gaze was piercing; I couldn't look him in the eyes. I thought, *Take it all in, this is one of the few times in your life you will meet a saint.*

I tried to look up at him, but I felt so unworthy to be in his presence that I knew if I continued to look into his eyes I was going to start crying, so I kept my eyes downcast. The last thing I wanted to do was start crying without even having taken his blessing yet.

When it was my turn to greet him I bent low, touched the ground, took his offered right hand, and reverently kissed it. Then I walked to my seat to listen to his homily. At that time I still did not understand Greek very well, and so I didn't catch a lot of what he said. He spoke for about an hour. Thankfully, Sr. Sarah translated it all for me immediately afterward.

Although he said many things, the following was the main theme of his homily and made the largest impact on me. He spoke about pain. The first thing he said was, "Christ did not come to abolish suffering, but to show us *how to suffer*. We must become like little Christs; He was crucified with His arms wide open, a sign of His love."

He said one-quarter of our world is suffering today from psychological illnesses—one of the main illnesses of our times. He said we must be refuges for all the people who suffer. He told us that Panagia is the joy of all who sorrow, and we must entreat her to allow us to become co-workers with her.

"If when we pray we have pain in our heart, and if we can have a few tears, we should entreat God to grant a little peace in the hearts of all those who suffer," he said.

He also told us we must always confess the pain we have in our hearts and never hold it in. In this way our spiritual fathers and mothers can help us and we can use the gift of pain, of suffering for another, to suffer in a proper way.

After he finished speaking, the two spiritual children who brought him helped him up and gave him his crutches. We all stood up to see him off.

Sr. Irene was standing beside me as we went out, and she said to me, "Where's Yianni when such a saint is here?" (That's what they called my husband—John in Greek).

"Do you think I could ask the Geronda for a spiritual word for John?" I asked.

"Yeah, why not? I'll ask Gerontissa if she thinks it's a good idea," she answered.

In a moment she returned, "Gerontissa said once he gets into the car and is sitting down you can ask him."

We all followed him to the parking lot as the two men assisted him on either side. On the way there, the elder stopped to take a break. Looking back at all of us, he said, "Are you all coming up to Golgotha with me?"

Once he was sitting in the car, Gerontissa gestured for me to come over. She told the elder, "This is Constantina, she's from Canada. She and her husband are students at the university in Thessaloniki. She wants to ask you something."

I took his blessing and he held my hand.

His hands are so soft, I noted to myself.

"Do you speak English?" I asked him in Greek.

"No. Do you speak French?" he asked me in French.

"No," I said.

And here I got myself into a funny scenario because of my limited experience with the Greek language. You see, when you want to ask someone for a "spiritual word" as we have come to call it in English, you ask for a spiritual *logo* in Greek. I, however, did not realize that. Since the Greek language has a variety of words that mean "word," I assumed I was suppose to say *lexi*. Asking for a spiritual *lexi* is like asking for a spiritual "term."

So, when I asked the elder for a "spiritual term" for my husband, he laughed and said, "Just one?"

And then his smile faded, he paused and looked straight ahead for a moment. Looking back at me he said, "Love."

And after another brief pause he said, "Love of Christ."

And then he smiled and released my hand. I thanked him, and Gerontissa closed the car door. All the nuns waved goodbye, some slightly bowed toward him, and some bent and touched the ground. That was my first experience of meeting this living saint.

Compliments Are Hard to Come By in a Monastery

IN HER EARLIER YEARS, GERONTISSA Philareti had been a fine iconographer, so I hoped to show her some of my drawings to get her opinion on them. I had gathered the last two years' worth of my work and brought them with me to the monastery.

It was summertime, which is usually very hot and humid, but every evening there was a welcome warm breeze at the monastery. Gerontissa and the nuns would sit together in the courtyard under the stars with the lights from the fountain on. This particular evening Gerontissa and some of the older nuns were sitting together around a folding table chopping vegetables. Since she was sitting down and had a free moment to speak with me, I took the opportunity to show her my drawings. She continued her cutting while I held up each drawing.

"Who is that?" she asked.

"It's Elder Paisios of the Holy Mountain," I said.

"It's not that good."

"I know, Gerontissa. It was one of my earlier sketches," I explained.

"Do you know who these monks are, Gerontissa?" I asked about a sketch of two hermits based on a photo I had seen.

"Yeah, but they look a bit cartoonish," she gently criticized.

I took out another sketch. "That one is so-so," she said.

I held up a drawing of Abbess Thaisia (St. John of Kronstadt's spiritual daughter) and she said, "You drew her well. She looks just like that!"

I showed her one of my later sketches of a hieromonk* she knew personally, and finally I received a smile. "Hold it up, hold it up! Look at that," she addressed the other nuns. "Look at the way his arms are crossed!" She laughed. "That looks exactly like him! *That* is a good one," she told me.

The Theotokos, When She Was Three Years Old, Was Led to the Lord

THE FOLLOWING STORY was very impressive to me. I heard it both from Sr. Thekla herself and from her mother. I was very moved to hear a story that so clearly demonstrates the Scriptures' claim, "Before I formed you in the womb I knew you" (Jeremiah 1:5).

The Theotokos, at the young age of three, ran up the stairs leading to the temple on her own. She did this because she desired, even then, to live solely for the Lord. So too, Sr. Thekla desired the monastic life. For even from an early age God's voice speaks "to those who are the called according to *His* purpose" (Rom. 8:28).

Sr. Thekla was four years old when she first visited the monastery with her grandmother and mother (who was a nominal Christian). One of the nuns was an old friend of her grandmother's, so they came to see the monastery and to stay the night.

Somehow, even at such a young age, not having met her before, the four-year-old Sr. Thekla was drawn to Gerontissa Philareti. When it came time for her to go to bed, she said, "I want to stay with Geron-tissa. Gerontissa, can I sleep in your bed?" Gerontissa laughed and patted her head.

Sr. Thekla's mother quickly interjected, "No, my child, you will stay with mommy!"

But at the persistence of the child, Sr. Paisia and Sr. Sophia allowed her to stay in their cell (which they shared). Sr. Thekla's mother, though quite hesitant and surprised at her daughter's boldness, agreed to allow her to stay with the nuns in their quarters.

I asked Sr. Thekla if she remembered anything from staying in the sisters' cell, but she said she only remembered going to sleep in one of the beds.

After that visit, she and her mother only visited once or twice more during Sr. Thekla's childhood. But through all her childhood and youth, Sr. Thekla remembered the monastery and yearned to live there. As an eight-year-old she saved her change in a piggy bank to give to the monastery, such a longing she possessed to live for Christ in the house of His saint.

When she was old enough to travel on the train alone, she began visiting the monastery. Thus her relentless pleading with Gerontissa to let her stay began. But Gerontissa continued to tell her, "Finish junior high, finish high school, finish university."

Every time Sr. Thekla finished a grade in school, she thought Gerontissa would allow her to stay, but it wasn't until she turned eighteen that, as a legal adult, she was able to stay. On receiving a letter from the monastery's spiritual father in which he gave her his blessing to become a novice, she went to Gerontissa and showed her the letter.

"Now will you let me stay?" she asked.

"Yes," Gerontissa responded.

It is clear that from an early age the Lord called to Sr. Thekla and she harkened unto His voice. As a child she saw something in the monastic life that spoke to her, and it stayed with her for fourteen years until she could finally call the monastery her own home and the abbess her own mother.

12

KNOT TWELVE

Paying a Tama

ONE SUNDAY AFTERNOON WHILE I was helping Sr. Theologia hose down the benches outside, I saw a woman crawling across the courtyard toward the church. She was wearing knee pads, and her husband was slowly walking beside her. I had never seen someone do something like this before, so I asked Sr. Theologia what the woman was doing.

"She's either here to pay a *tama* to the saint or to ask him for something," she answered.

I cannot imagine doing something like that, I thought.

"What is a tama?" I asked.

"You know, an oblation," Sr. Theologia said.

"You mean like a vow or a promise?" I asked.

"Yes," she said. "Usually couples who cannot conceive a child come and ask the saint to give them a child, and out of gratitude they offer something to the saint in return. The patron of the monastery has granted a lot of people's requests for children. Afterward, a lot of people baptize those children here. We'll have to ask the woman if the saint granted her request, because we record the miracles he works."

I do not know how common it is for Orthodox Christians outside of Orthodox countries to do tamas, but in Greece they are very common. Since that day when I saw the woman crawl across the stone courtyard, I have seen and read about many more tamas.

Once a tama is granted—or even before it is granted—the person fulfills his vow. Contrary to outward appearance, this is not a business transaction, nor a method of bribery. A person who requests something of the saint, or of the Mother of God or of God, needs to be sincere and at least desire to lead a spiritual life. Those who treat tamas as some sort of magical means of getting what they want do not approach the saint with the appropriate disposition.

There is a great deal of historical and traditional precedent for tamas. The Prophet Samuel's mother promised if God gave her a child she would allow her child to live in the temple. St. Joachim and St. Anna did a similar thing with the Virgin Mary. They gave her up to the temple as "payment" for their request having been granted. St. Gregory the Theologian made a tama when he was on a boat in a storm and feared for his life. He told the Lord if He preserved him he would become a monk, and he fulfilled that vow.

In one of the chapels at St. Nektarios's monastery in Aegina, the entire ceiling has oil lamps hanging from it. They were all gifts to the saint for having heeded the faithful's prayers and requests. Many icons have gold chains, rings, and crosses hung before them—often offered as tokens of gratitude to the saint. Ultimately tamas are simply a sign of reverence and gratitude.

A tama can be anything from giving your favorite gold cross to the saint's icon, to dedicating your child to God, in the case of the Prophet Samuel's mother, Hannah. It can be taking on a certain amount of extra fasting or prayers, or giving money to a church or monastery. There are no rules about these things. It depends on the inclination of the individual's heart; it can be as small or as great a vow as one desires. The most important thing is simply that we fulfill our promises.

The woman I saw that day had come, crawling on her knees, to beg the saint to pray for her to conceive a child. The nuns in the church advised her to ask Gerontissa Philareti for a piece of rope—blessed on the miracle-working icon of the saint—which she kept to give to the faithful. This rope, similar to the rope given to the faithful blessed on the Holy Belt of the Mother of God,* is worn by women around their waist until they are able to conceive. The couple is also encouraged to fast and abstain for a time and then, with prayer, come together.

I don't know what became of the couple or whether they eventually conceived, but I'm sure in good time the Lord granted their request according to His all-good will.

Leaving My Handprint in a Historical Monastery

THERE IS MUCH TALK of "walking the path less trodden" and leaving our "mark" on the world in our modern-day society. We are encouraged not merely to follow in the footsteps of those that have walked before us but to offer something new, something unique, something of our own individual selves. I did just that in the museum at the monastery. Of course it was completely unintentional and rather embarrassing, but it does guarantee one thing: My individual handprint has left a mark and will remain in that historical monastery.

After we visited the monastery two or three times when a general cleaning was taking place, it became a running joke that whenever my husband and I visited a general cleaning of some large room or area would be done. I remember when we helped dust every single item in the bookstore. We put them aside so we could clean the surfaces of the shelves and table tops, dusted all the individual items, and put them back in place. At other times we would dust down all the different things in the museum with a wet cloth and dry them.

This particular time Sr. Seraphima was pleased to have us put olive oil on every metal item in the museum. One item after another we covered in oil to help preserve them. We were almost finished when we had to oil the metal part of a machine that had a conveyer belt attached to it. As I knelt down low to oil the underside of the machine, I rested my hand on the conveyer belt, and getting up, to my horror, I realized I had left an oily handprint on the canvas belt. I was mortified. What was I going to tell Sr. Seraphima? Out of stupidity I put my oily hand on the two-hundred-year-old conveyer belt?

I sheepishly confessed my negligence, and she and Sr. Philothei worked out a way to maneuver the belt so that my handprint was no longer visible. "Well, at least my handprint will always be here in the monastery!" I teased them.

Sixteen and a Half Kilos of Incense and a Lesson

I HAD SPOKEN WITH SR. SARAH on the telephone to tell her we would like to come out to the monastery at some point and to ask her if my brother and sister-in-law could come with us. She and

I were excited because she had told me they needed to make lots of incense, and she knew we wanted to learn how to make it, so we were going to ask Gerontissa and Sr. Paisia if we could make incense on our planned visit.

They gladly agreed to have us come out, so we packed up and arrived the next afternoon. As soon as we arrived, they served us lunch. The delicious food the sisters serve us pilgrims makes us feel as if we're paid for our work there.

Straight after breakfast the next morning we were to join Sr. Sarah and Sr. Euphemia in the incense workshop. They had been so busy in the last year they had hardly had any time to make incense, so a dozen kilos of three or four different aromas were on the schedule to be made.

The first day alone, we worked from ten in the morning until eleven at night, with a two-hour break around two in the afternoon and a quick supper at eight. That day we made eight kilos. Boy, were our hands sore! So much rolling out of the incense in order to cut it into small rectangular shapes and then mold them into balls!

We prayed while we worked, sang hymns, and tried to keep at least some silence. The next day the four of us (not including the nuns) decided it would be a safer and better idea to wear masks since we were working with powder magnesium. Coincidentally my light-headedness from the day before didn't return. (In Greece it's very common for workers to be seen without glasses to protect their eyes, gloves to protect their hands, or masks to protect their lungs. Sometimes you just have to look away when you see a city worker using a flaming torch to do fine work without any eye protection.)

One afternoon during our work, I went across the courtyard to get something out of the kitchen, and I saw a visiting young woman in the reception area wearing a headscarf. She was accompanying a priest, a child, and an older gentleman. I was surprised because I had never seen Greek pilgrims wear headscarves in a Greek monastery before (except in the church). Overcome with curiosity, when I returned to the workroom I said to the sisters, "There's a young woman over there with a priest, and she's wearing a headscarf. Where do you suppose she is from? Do you think she's Greek?"

"I don't know," Sr. Euphemia said, humoring me. "We'll have to find out."

About half an hour later, Sr. Sarah had to go over to the kitchen, so I told her, "Try to find out who that woman is." She smiled.

My obvious curiosity must have triggered a memory in Sr. Euphemia because she started laughing.

"You know, Geronda teases us and says that women are so curious that you can never tell them a secret because they'll go and tell it!"

I laughed. "Well, if I'm any indication, he's right. I'm so horribly curious."

"Once while he was visiting us, a bus full of pilgrims from Kozani came. Later that day we all went to get his blessing and he put each nun to the test:

"'Irene, where was that bus of pilgrims from?'

"'Oh, I don't know Geronda, I didn't think to ask,' she answered.

"To the next nun he said, 'Joanna, where was that bus from, do you know?'

"'No, Geronda,' she answered.

"He asked this question to every nun until finally someone said, 'Geronda, I know where they were from, Kozani. I spoke with some of the women.'

"'Oh, you did, did you?' he asked.

"And then he proceeded to teach us not to ask many questions and to avoid giving in to curiosity about other people or places," she finished with her characteristic smile.

"Oh man," I said, smiling and shaking my head, "I'm so bad."

Unfortunately, Sr. Euphemia's story didn't fix my problem. Two days later there was a memorial service after the Divine Liturgy, and she told me afterward it was for a young man who had died. I asked her how and she said, "I don't know, but I'll find out."

I broke down laughing, realizing my folly and remembering the story she had just told me days before. I begged her not to ask, since I would be turning her into an information hound too.

Her story has stayed with me (even if I temporarily forget it), and whenever I want to find something out that is superfluous, I try to temper my curiosity with the elder's words. This was the nuns' gentle way of molding me, though hard as stone, into a better Christian. However, I never felt *taught* by them.

I never felt as though they looked at me as someone who needed to learn something. I only ever felt loved by them. This is why I was never embarrassed by all the more serious mistakes I made, like revealing my unrestrained curiosity to them. I felt like I was able to show them my less attractive traits and habits, and still they loved me and cared for me. When they told me stories that helped me or corrected me, I always felt that I merely triggered their memory about something interesting, humorous, or beneficial. I never felt as though they treated me as inferior, but as their friend and equal.

In our modern, mostly democratic world this seems insignificant, but it is telling. Monastics are a light for us in the world. They are the "SWAT team" of Christianity, as my professor used to say. And yet, they always willingly condescended to raise me up, to try to make me into the Christian I ought to have been. Their humble disposition made outright teaching unnecessary; I was taught by their love.

KNOT THIRTEEN

The Providence of God

S R. SARAH AND I WERE in the storage room unpacking some boxes that had been delivered that day with icons for the bookstore. We had to organize all the icons in the new shelving unit, replenish the old stock, and add the new. So she handed me a walkie-talkie and told me, "I'll go to the other storage room and collect the icons we need to restock these shelves. With the walkie-talkie I'll ask you which ones we need and lay them aside to bring them up."

Before long I was thoroughly enjoying myself communicating with the walkie-talkies and telling her which and how many icons we needed of St. Haralambos, All-Saints, the Dormition, and many others. Once we finished, we started restocking the shelves with the new order of icons and the ones Sr. Sarah brought over from storage.

While I was going through the new stock, organizing the icons into piles according to the scenes or saints depicted, I noticed one medium-sized icon that was the only one of its kind in the shipment. It was a female saint and the name read, "Harikleia." I had never heard of this saint, so I asked Sr. Sarah who it was.

"I don't know," she said. "And it's not on the order sheet. I have no idea why it's with this shipment. Let's put it aside and we'll ask Sr. Seraphima about it later. Maybe she ordered it for someone who requested it in particular."

We laid it aside and continued organizing the icons.

Later that day, a couple I had met a few times in Thessaloniki arrived for Vespers with their one-year-old daughter, Haroula. After the service I sat with them for some time. Sophia, the child's mother, mentioned she would like to look around the bookstore, so Sr. Sarah accompanied her. I stayed with Jason, and the conversation turned to their daughter.

I asked which saint they had named her after, and he said: "Her proper name is Harikleia. St. Harikleia was one of the forty virgin martyrs. We celebrate her feast day on September 1. She and the other virgin martyrs lived in Adrianopoulos, Thrace, in northeastern Greece. But unfortunately we have never been able to find an icon of her."

"What did you say?" I asked dumbfounded. "What was the saint's name?"

"Harikleia," he answered.

"Oh my goodness, I think we just unpacked an icon of her in the storage room!" I said. "When Sr. Sarah comes back, we'll ask if you can buy it."

Soon afterward Sr. Sarah and Sophia returned. "Sarah, you know that icon we laid aside today—"

"Yeah," she cut me off, "I'm going to go get it and see if they can buy it, because Sophia just told me they don't have an icon of the baby's saint."

Sr. Sarah went to ask Sr. Seraphima about it in case it was meant for someone else, but according to the will of God, it was sent by mistake. The couple was able to take it and for the first time venerate the child's namesake.

Truly, there are no coincidences in this life. St. Harikleia was just waiting to be found. God is great in His saints!

Blessed Are They Who Hunger and Thirst *after Righteousness*

ONE THING I DON'T THINK most pilgrims or visitors realize is that the monastery, like monasteries in general, suffers financially. Following in the monastic tradition of self-sacrifice and hospitality, the nuns offer a plethora of food, sweets, coffee, and anything else that is available to their guests whenever they can. But secretly they barely have enough money to run the monastery and do not dress their own table with half as much food as they prepare for the guests.

In Greece lunch is the largest meal of the day. So, on a Sunday afternoon, for instance, for about ten visitors, you may find two plates of roasted potatoes or fries, two salads, two bowls of olives, two baskets of bread, caviar dip, side dishes with cooked vegetables, a main course on everyone's own individual plate, and two plates of sweets. This leads us visitors to assume that the nuns eat similarly. But having stayed there often enough and having become very close to the sisters, I know they do not eat the way they feed us visitors. While a table of a dozen guests may have two plates with a mound of fried fish piled on top of each, the nuns may only have one small fish apiece. They believe it is better for them to go without in order for guests to have more.

Now, if most people who visit the monastery knew this, they would most certainly be dismayed and would not want the nuns to have less than they have, but the sisters, out of *philotimo*,* do not want them to know this. I mention it here because I think it is a common misunderstanding. When we visit some monasteries, we look around at the food, the well-kept grounds, and the ornately decorated chapels, and we automatically assume the monastery has a lot of money. More often than not, they are struggling to make ends meet but selflessly offer all they have to beautify the temple of the Lord and give to the guests. They want pilgrims to visit the monastery and leave feeling spiritually and physically nourished.

It would soften a heart of stone to know just how much these blessed ones, who have given up everything—family, friends, careers, secular comforts like movies, coffee shops, and time to oneself—do for us in the world, who seemingly lack nothing. They do all of this out of true devotion to the commandments of Christ. They live a secluded and obscure life, never letting their "left hand know what their right hand is doing" (Matt. 6:3).

They, like all monastics, live for Christ in the known outward manners of obedience, chastity, and poverty, but they also follow Him in hidden ways, which makes their sacrifice all the more praiseworthy. They are prime examples of Abraham's hospitality and of following the spirit of the law. "And whoever compels you to go one mile, go with him two" (Matt. 5:41). They unknowingly encourage us by their example to give of ourselves secretly so that we can be rewarded openly, by being permitted to live with Christ, when He comes in His Kingdom.

An English Pilgrim

ONE AFTERNOON, WHILE ENJOYING ONE of the said meals at the monastery, I met an English woman who had married a Greek man. She had lived in Greece for some years but had remained an unchurched Anglican. She told me that gradually her husband started becoming more pious and would visit the Holy Mountain with friends. This, in turn, had an effect on their family.

During one of his trips, he and a friend visited the renowned Elder Paisios the Athonite (+1994). The wife was pregnant at the time with their first child, and while staying at home alone, she continually watched Greek soap operas because she was bored. As soon as Elder Paisios laid eyes on the men, before they could even get a word out, he said, "You tell that pregnant wife of yours to turn off the television!"

When her husband called her that day, he told her, "Geronda Paisios told me to tell you to turn the television off and not watch it so much."

"Once my husband returned from Mount Athos, we got rid of the television altogether and started playing chess," she said, laughing.

Some years later, when her children grew older, they started asking her why she didn't come to church or communion with them. She started taking Orthodoxy more seriously and looking into it more closely. She developed a relationship with a well-known Athonite spiritual father at Xerapotamou Monastery, and he advised her and her husband to start visiting Gerontissa Philareti's monastery.

After some time, she told her spiritual father she wanted to be baptized, and he suggested she ask Gerontissa to be her godmother. She was baptized at the monastery, she and her husband continued to grow in their faith, and they became a lovely pious family.

KNOT THIRTEEN

Forgiveness of Sins

IT WAS A HOT JULY afternoon and Sr. Marina was outside vacuuming the courtyard, making sure the smooth stones were free of dirt and dust. I was in the kitchen helping the sisters make tuna-rice stuffed zucchinis. Sr. Lydia was also in the kitchen making juice out of the watermelon that was beginning to turn. She placed a steel cup of juice and one of water on a small tray.

"Do you want to take this to Marina?" she asked me, holding out the tray.

I took the tray and walked out into the courtyard. When Sr. Marina saw me, she turned off the vacuum and pulled off the large straw sun hat she was wearing.

"This is for you," I said, placing the tray down on the steps leading into the sitting area around the fountain.

"*Theos schores sou* [may God forgive your sins], Constantina," she said. Taking the watermelon juice and crossing herself, she downed half the cup. "May God grant you your every good desire," she said, placing the steel cup down on the tray.

This was the monastic way of saying "thank you." They give much more than simple thanksgiving; they give you the hope that God will forgive your sins. We respond with, "Amen," so be it. Since forgiveness of our sins is the greatest thing we can acquire in this life, the simple Greek phrase, *Theos schores sou*, is a penetrating prayer.

Another instance in which this phrase captured my attention was when I witnessed the following. Sr. Monica and Sr. Margaret's mother, Mrs. Olga, had come out to the monastery to patch up some of the nuns' clothes. The nuns never threw away anything that could be mended, and especially not their original rasso. This is why monastic work clothing is often a variety of blues and grays. For days Mrs. Olga had been bent over sewing up holes, mending hemlines, and reattaching buttons.

One afternoon, after finishing up our own separate tasks, we sat down together in the guest dining hall for lunch. Sr. Raphaela came in to ask if Mrs. Olga had finished mending her vest.

"Here it is," Mrs. Olga said, handing Sr. Raphaela her folded vest.

"*Theos schores sou*, Mrs. Olga!" Sr. Raphaela exclaimed.

"No, no, it was nothing," Mrs. Olga said, shaking her head and shying away from accepting what she perceived to be common thanks.

"Mrs. Olga, what 'nothing'? I didn't say 'thank you,' I said that I hope God will forgive your sins," Sr. Raphaela said, reminding Mrs. Olga that thanksgiving and a prayer for one's forgiveness are very different. The former puts the emphasis on the individual, while the latter puts the emphasis on God granting something to the individual for his or her good works.

After witnessing that conversation, I became careful to respond affirmatively whenever the nuns said *Theos schores sou* to me.

God willing, every good deed we do or word we utter will be accounted to us for forgiveness of our sins on that terrible Day of Judgment.

Forgiveness is not only something monastics wish for others, it is something they often ask for as well. Many times on parting with a monk or nun, he or she will say, "And please forgive me if I said or did anything that offended you."

In the beginning, this would take me by surprise and made me feel awkward, because I wasn't sure if they thought they had offended me, or if they were merely being careful to avoid cause for hard feelings. After time I grew accustomed to monastics' request for forgiveness and even managed to ask for it a few times myself.

14

KNOT FOURTEEN

Temptation in the Garden

ONCE A YEAR THE MONASTERY has a priest come and serve Divine Liturgy for forty consecutive days. The sisters always choose a less busy time of year when a priest is more likely to be available. This particular year about which I am speaking, they chose to have their forty-day Liturgy served during the Apostles' fast.

Every time they had their forty-day Liturgy, some burdensome temptation came with it. So, although it was unfortunate, it was not at all surprising when the water in the stream that runs alongside the outer walls of the monastery rose quite suddenly due to some problem with the dam downstream.

Not only did the water rise, but it became so forceful that it broke the stone wall that was attached to the culvert which guided the water under the road and away from the garden. On breaking the wall, the water rushed straight ahead and right through the middle of the garden. It not only destroyed the whole middle section of the upper garden, but it ran on over the side of the bank and down into the lower garden and ruined that one as well.

The nuns were understandably dismayed by this, but exhibited characteristic patience. They knew that where grace is, temptation is also. The evil one's hatred knows no bounds, but then again neither does the grace of God, and ultimately God is always victorious.

A Visit from Elder Isidoros the Blind

ELDER ISIDOROS IS A BLIND MONK from Philotheou Monastery. He is roughly in his late seventies now and has been a monk for about thirty-five years. He spent his first years as a monastic at the monastery of Xerapotamou and later moved to the monastery of Philotheou.

I had the great blessing of meeting him a few times. I went to the monastery to help out with some work. On arriving I walked into one of the small workrooms near the kitchen to put my bags down—since the sisters had not yet told me which guestroom I would be staying in. When I walked in, I saw a monk sitting on a chair speaking with a woman. I noticed immediately that he was blind, and even though I knew he wasn't a priest, in keeping with the Greek custom, I took his blessing.

In Greece whether or not a monk is a priest, and especially if he is older, you take his blessing by kissing his hand. The same is done with older nuns; it's a gesture of respect. Although I never kissed any of the nuns' hands at the monastery except for Gerontissa Phila-reti's, out in the world many people will take the blessing of an older monk or nun when they meet them. Or, I should say, they'll try to, but often the monastic pulls his or her hand away out of humility.

After I took the elder's blessing and he greeted me, I went into the kitchen to say hello to the sisters. I asked Sr. Sarah who the monk was, and she said his name was Fr. Isidoros.

"You've met him here before, haven't you?" she asked.

"No, but Katerina and Anna told me a lot about him," I answered.

I had heard many stories about him from two young women I met from Athens who were his spiritual children. They told me so many stories about the miracles he worked, the people he helped, the spiritual foresight he had, and how *funny* he was, that I could hardly recall half of them. I was very pleased to hear that was the monk whose blessing I had taken, especially since he was to leave for the Holy Mountain early the next morning.

That day and well into the night, until the nuns turned the phones off around eleven PM, they rang nearly non-stop. Finally I asked Sr. Xenia, "What's going on today? Why are the phones ringing so much?"

"People found out the papouli is staying here and they are calling to speak with him," she said.

"That many people are calling him?"

"Yes, Constantina. He has many spiritual children and helps a lot of people. He has healed tons of people from cancer too. He goes to Athens a few times a year, and recently there were so many people lined up to see him, the line went from one neighborhood into another and the police showed up to make sure everything was all right," she answered.

The next morning, I sat down to have breakfast and the phone rang. Sure enough it was for the papouli. "He already left for the Holy Mountain," I overheard Sr. Marina telling the person on the line. "But we just heard that he will be returning. Due to the weather the boat can't leave."

I was sorting olives with some of the sisters and a few women from the village when Elder Isidoros came in with Sr. Raphaela guiding him. She sat him down in the middle of us, gave him a bowl, and put a large garbage bag on either side of him. He was going to separate the olives from the twigs and leaves as we were doing.

The women were so excited to have him there that they each wanted to sit beside him. Once everyone was settled I asked him if he could speak to us about some things.

"No, but if you want to ask me some things I will answer," he said.

Questions came up as we worked away sorting the black from the green olives, those for the olive press and those for eating. While we worked we spoke about many things, and here are some of the things we learned. Kalliopi spoke first: "Papouli, I have a really bad memory and can't remember anything. No matter what I do I forget very easily. I'm really stupid like that."

"Yeah, that's it!" the elder said, playing along. "That's what you should call yourself—stupid!" he said, smiling.

Kalliopi laughed. "Isn't there anything I can do to help myself have a better memory?"

"The only thing that matters is humility. It doesn't matter whether we remember things or not, we just need humility," the elder said seriously.

"Geronda," I said, "if, God willing, my husband and I return to Canada and he becomes a priest, besides frequent Divine Liturgies and services every day, what can we do to bring Orthodoxy to the people?"

"The first thing you should do is visit the sick in the hospitals. Speak to them and visit them. That is what Christ did first, He healed the sick. Then people will come," he said.

"Papouli, what is the difference between regret and repentance?" one of the other women asked.

"Bah! Regret! We don't care about regret! The Christian cares about repentance. Forget regret!" he responded.

A little while later he started speaking about Jerusalem, about all the holy sites there and the grace they contain. "Have any of you been to the holy sites in Jerusalem?" he asked.

"Yes, I have," one of the women answered.

"And?" the elder asked. "How was it? How did you feel?"

"Full of peace, and grace, and ..." The woman struggled to find words.

"And it's indescribable, isn't it?" the elder said, getting excited.

He then proceeded to describe the different places in the Holy Land and what they were like. He described some things with a lot of detail, to the extent that Kalliopi and I would glance at each other with suspicion.

"And how do *you* know what it looks like there, Papouli?" she asked him. But he didn't respond.

"Geronda, I have another question," I said. "What is a practical way to avoid judging our neighbor?"

"That's a very good question! A very good question! Hold on! Excuse me but, when someone calls us a liar or a thief, is there anyone among us who didn't lie once in their life? Who didn't steal something at least once?"

"No, Papouli," we all answered.

"Then, we are what they call us!" he said, giving a very nice answer, if a little off topic.

Someone else asked about feeling unworthy to receive Holy Communion: "Even though I fast and do the preparation prayers, sometimes I still feel so unworthy I think I shouldn't receive."

"No, we don't pay any attention to how we feel. No attention at all," the elder advised.

"Papouli, why don't you tell us something about the Panagia?" I asked.

He paused for quite some time. "You have to be by yourself for me to tell you about her," he said quietly. "Come to my cell tonight and I will speak to you about her."

"May it be blessed, Geronda," I said. But this special conversation is worthy of its own story, which I will share with you later.

Periodically the elder would say, "Whatever you want to ask me, just ask, okay?"

And sometimes after he said something funny he would become very serious and say, "I'm not upsetting you, am I?"

In this way he revealed how simple and sensitive he was. Naturally he was funny in his responses and quips, but he was also careful not to offend anyone. At some point one of the women said something funny, and he took a handful of leaves and threw them at her, and he was actually on target! We all laughed hard, and he said, "You see how a person laughs when the soul is free? You see? When the soul is free you can laugh!"

Due to the poor weather, the elder ended up staying another four days. I had the great honor of spending time with him, speaking with him, and helping him around the monastery. And I was taught many more important lessons.

My Big Brother

MANY OF THE NUNS HAD different spiritual fathers before coming to the monastery. However, once they entered the monastery, they not only left behind their family according to the flesh but also their family according to the spirit.

It's not that a monastic forgets his or her family or stops loving and praying for them. Rather, just as a man leaves his father and mother and joins with his wife, forming a new family, so the monastic leaves behind her old family to join a new family. The abbess becomes her mother, the sisterhood her siblings, and the spiritual father of the monastery her father.

Usually, but not always, monastics are permitted to visit with their family, call them, write to them, and continue to treat them as family. However, this is all done with the spiritual benefit of the monastic and his or her family in mind.

Sometimes it is better for silence to take the place of communication when things are not on the best of terms. At other times the family may choose not to speak with the monastic, and the monk or nun has the obedience of keeping up the communication so the family does not become embittered. These are pastoral matters. One thing that is clear, though, is the new spiritual family has priority, just as the husband's newly formed family does.

One afternoon Gerontissa Philareti happened to enter one of the novice's cells. In a frame sitting on a shelf along with framed photos of herself and the monastery's spiritual father, Gerontissa saw a photograph of this sister's spiritual father from the world. Gerontissa knew this priest well—in fact, they were very close and spoke regularly on the telephone. However, to make a point, she asked, "Who is that?"

The novice thought quickly. "It's my big brother," she said. Answering this way, she showed that she no longer viewed him as her spiritual father but rather as a co-struggler, since he shared the monastery's spiritual father.

"Put it away," Gerontissa told her.

She did this to protect the novice. Although Gerontissa allowed her to keep the photograph, she made it clear what family the novice had left behind and what family she had recently joined.

KNOT FIFTEEN

It Is Truly Meet to Call Her Blessed, Even While Sewing

AS I HAVE ALREADY MENTIONED, the monastery has a small olive orchard from which the sisters gather their olives. When God grants them a good harvest, they also have a portion of their olives pressed for oil. One hot week in the summer, the abbess's aunt was visiting in order to help the sisterhood with any sewing that needed to be done. It was decided that it was time for the sisters to mend the olive net, since Gerontissa's aunt could offer her assistance.

Her name was Mrs. Dina, and I loved her very much. She, although of a mature age, was afraid of the dark and of sleeping alone. So I got moved out of my room to stay with her so she wouldn't be afraid. When Sr. Marina came to tell me I needed to stay with Mrs. Dina because she was afraid of the dark, we both giggled, thinking about a grown woman being afraid of the dark. Did I ever suffer for that stupid laughter!

After I had stayed a few days with Mrs. Dina, one of her nieces arrived, so they stayed together and I returned to my room. That night, all alone in my room, I couldn't sleep, and a bizarre fear took hold of me. I was petrified by every sound. I was so frightened I just lay under my sheets, praying.

The next day I went straight to Sr. Marina. "Last night I couldn't sleep—I was too terrified!"

"Why?" she asked, concerned.

"I don't know, but I think it's because I laughed at Mrs. Dina!"

This made Sr. Marina laugh pretty hard. "No, Constantina!"

When Gerontissa came into the kitchen, Sr. Marina, amused that I thought I was being punished for my laughter, told Gerontissa of my unexplainable fear the night before.

"Constantina, why were you afraid last night?" Gerontissa asked in her characteristic soft and quiet voice, all the while smiling.

"I don't know, Gerontissa, maybe because I laughed at Mrs. Dina for being afraid of the dark."

Her response was just laughter.

During these days a group of us were assigned to help Mrs. Dina mend all the holes in the twelve-meter-by-three-meter olive net, which had been torn in various spots over the years by thorns and bushes. Eight of us sewed together: Sr. Sarah, Sr. Marina, Sr. Xenia, Sr. Theologia, Sr. Monica, Sr. Agathi, Sr. Akakia, and I.

This seemingly insignificant event has been one of my dearest memories of all my visits to the monastery. We sat around the sewing room spread out at first, sitting on upside down crates, each working away at the larger holes while Mrs. Dina sewed up the smaller ones. As the days went on and the sections needing sewing became smaller, we had to continually move closer together. By the last day, we were in such a small huddle that all of our knees were touching.

During those hot summer days, the nuns working in the kitchen would bring us freshly squeezed juice and watermelon to keep us hydrated. While sewing we prayed the Akathist hymn together, told spiritual stories we had read in books or heard in homilies, said the Jesus Prayer, of course, and sang different hymns and occasional Greek folk songs like "Agia Sophia." That was one of my personal favorites. It is about some Greeks overlooking Constantinople from a mountain after the Turkish takeover and longing for the return of the cathedral of Agia Sophia to Christendom.

One day while we were sewing, I mentioned to Sr. Monica—who was a chanter—that I loved the hymn *Axion Estin* (It is Truly Meet) very much. I asked her to sing it for us, and she did. It turned out Mrs. Dina also must have loved that hymn very much, because she was so moved by Sr. Monica's chanting that she started to cry. At the same time she put her hand to her nose. "My nose is bleeding!"

"Mrs. Dina, what happened?" Sr. Monica asked.

"It's from emotion," Mrs. Dina answered, still teary-eyed and getting a tissue.

Now, you are probably thinking about how strange that is, but if you know Greeks well you already know they are very emotional people. I remember being at the *ahondariki* (church hall) when our priest read a poem in honor of mothers. He got so choked with emotion he had to pause many times in the course of the poem, and at the end at least half a dozen people, men and women, were wiping the tears off their faces. Oh, to have such sensitive hearts—it's a true gift!

Sharing Spiritual Stories

SOME OF THE STORIES THE NUNS TOLD ME during those days while we sewed the olive net will always stay with me. I heard some truly amazing things during that week of work.

After singing *Agia Sophia*, I told them about my trip with my husband to Constantinople earlier that summer, and they told me about Patriarch Gennadios Scholarios. He was the first Patriarch after the city fell.

After the Turks took over Constantinople, the ruling Sultan Mehmed II, who led the capture of the city, had a recurring dream about a hand with five fingers. Upset that neither he nor any other Muslim could decipher its meaning, the Sultan sent out his men to find the monk Gennadios, who was renowned for his insight into things of a spiritual nature. Once they found him, the men asked monk Gennadios to interpret the Sultan's dream. Gennadios agreed but said he needed to fast and pray for several days before he would be able to interpret it.

After fasting and praying, he was informed by God what the dream meant. The hand with five fingers the Sultan continually saw in his dream represented five faithful Christians—the five faithful Christians Constantinople did *not* have living in it at the time of its collapse.

"If there had been only five faithful Christians in Constantinople, God would not have allowed it to be captured by you," monk Gennadios explained to the Sultan.

Relieved to finally have his dream interpreted, Sultan Mehmed II promised not to persecute the Christians and to make Gennadios the leader of his people. The Sultan honored his promise. Thus, monk Gennadios became the first Ecumenical Patriarch after the fall of the city.

Later in his life, Patriarch Gennadios came to live out his days and be buried in a monastery in Northern Greece, which I have visited a few times.

Imagine, I thought to myself, *if back then there weren't even five faithful Christians in Constantinople, how many would God find in our cities today?*

Sr. Sarah shared a story with us that Sr. Paisia had told some of the nuns just after news came that Sr. Christodora's cancer had returned. Sr. Paisia called it a "dream," but as Sr. Sarah pointed out, "You know, the kind of *dreams* holy people see while they are praying."

Sr. Paisia said she was walking in a large field and suddenly turned to see a large, fierce, black dog running towards her. She started running to get away from it since it was heading directly for her. She perceived it wanted to devour her. She ran as hard and as fast as she could, all the while feeling the dog's breath on the back of her legs—it was so close to her.

Just as she was beginning to lose hope of escaping the attack of this vicious animal, she saw a tall man on the other side of the field encouraging her. He had curly hair as St. George does in his icons, was very tall, and was wearing long robes. As she ran he beckoned for her, and as soon as she got close enough, he opened up his cloak and hid her within its folds. When she opened the cloak to see outside, the dog's face was there snarling at her.

Somehow—Sr. Sarah didn't really remember how—the tall man got rid of the dog and told Sr. Paisia it was okay to come out. He was her guardian angel, and he pointed to a nearby city on a hill. "Do you see that large palace?" he asked. "That belongs to your spiritual father. Your former abbess lives there, along with some of the other nuns from your sisterhood who fell asleep in the Lord. All you have to do is struggle and someday you'll go to live there as well."

This is what Sr. Sarah told us. Sr. Paisia had told it to some of the nuns in order to give them hope in the midst of their trial. It seems even monastics can falter when faced with difficulties and require encouragement at times.

SR. XENIA TOLD ME ABOUT her mother, a pious woman who had experienced many amazing things. She was an ascetic in the world; every year for the first six days of Great Lent she would abstain from all food and drink until the evening, when she would simply have a Greek coffee and a small piece of bread. Today most monastics and some laity fast like this—from all food and drink—for the first three days of Great Lent. Sr. Xenia's mother, however, wanted to follow in the footsteps of earlier ascetics who kept a longer strict fast. More impressive still, she was the mother of eight children!

Sr. Xenia's father, a priest, used to call her at the monastery sometimes and say, "Tell your mother she needs to eat; she's not eating enough!"

"*Baba* [Dad], what can I tell her? Since her spiritual father gave her a blessing, there's nothing I can say!" Sr. Xenia would answer.

Sr. Xenia also told me the following miracle that happened through her mother's supplication to a beloved saint.

It was Bright Tuesday and Sr. Xenia's mother had given birth to twins, but unfortunately the baby boy was not very healthy, and due to some complication the doctors thought he would not be able to walk. The mother prayed fervently to St. Nektarios to heal her child. She made a tama to him in the hope that he would grant her request and heal her child.

That same day an old, short, white-haired priest came into her hospital room and asked her, "What will you name the children?"

She told him which names she had in mind. He said, "But it's

Pascha—you must name one of them after the Resurrection!" (In Greek, the word *anastasi*, "resurrection," is used as the name Anastasios for a boy and Anastasia for a girl.)

"But Father, I wanted to name the children something else," she said, not yet realizing to whom she was speaking.

"You should name one of them in honor of the Resurrection," he advised and turned to leave.

Afterward she decided to heed the advice of the old priest and named the girl Anastasia and the boy Nektarios since, through the intercession of the saint, the child had become well.

About two years later, she took the children to St. Nektarios's monastery in Aegina to "pay" the tama she'd made. Since the saint worked the miracle for the child, she got him to walk on his own up the winding, well-trodden path to the monastery. When the nun receiving the visitors at the gate saw the children, she asked, "What are their names?"

The mother told her, "Nektarios and Anastasia."

When the nun heard this, she smiled and said, "Really? Did you know St. Nektarios's name was Anastasios before he became a monk?"

And it was at this moment the mother realized the old priest who had visited her in the hospital was St. Nektarios himself. She glorified God who is great in His saints!

MRS. DINA ALSO SHARED WITH US an encounter she had with a saint while she was in the hospital for heart surgery. She needed to have open heart surgery but was very anxious and afraid it would go badly. So she fervently prayed to St. Panteleimon the Unmercenary.

While she was in the hospital awaiting her surgery, a tall young man wearing green scrubs came to the doorway. Initially Mrs. Dina thought he was the doctor. However, he acted in a rather peculiar way. He stretched out his arm toward her and waved it up and down in the air a few times. Before she could say anything, he turned to leave, but as he was exiting a stream of light followed behind him. It was then that Mrs. Dina realized it was St. Panteleimon. She felt at peace, and the surgery was a success.

16

KNOT SIXTEEN

A Blessed Life

SINCE THE UNIVERSITY WAS ON HOLIDAY for Holy and Bright Week, we decided to take the opportunity to visit the sisters after Pascha. There was another visitor, Anne, who had come from Australia for two weeks and was to be flying out of Thessaloniki that same afternoon. She was the sister of Sr. Nektaria.

As she was saying goodbye to the nuns, she started crying. It was clearly difficult for her to leave; she had bonded and become close to them. The nuns comforted her, wished her a good trip back, and told her not to let so much time pass before visiting the next time.

Watching all of this, I began to reflect that a monastery is a refuge for us all. It offers routine, prayer life, companionship, and support. In the world it's hard to find these things, and if one is fortunate enough to find them, they often don't last.

The monastery is an image of what true Christian life should be. Trials and temptations exist, but they are faced within community, not on one's own—just as the parish is meant to be when it functions properly. I think this is why Anne cried.

Once Anne left, I said to Sr. Xenia, "The monastic life really is a blessed life."

She, in a matter-of-fact tone, as though what I said didn't warrant any explanation, said, "Yeah, I know. That's why everyone cries when they leave here. If you think Anne was bad, you should've seen Sr. Nektaria's brother. He could barely get on the airplane!"

As Many as Were Baptized into Christ

MANY PEOPLE COME to the monastery to baptize their children—especially those who conceived through the intercession of the patron saint of the monastery. Others come because it is a beautiful place for baptism pictures. Whatever the reason, the result is the same: A newly illumined person becomes a member of the Body of Christ, granting him or her the possibility of entering the Kingdom of Heaven.

After a baptism one Sunday afternoon, the mother of the newly illumined baby went to sit with Gerontissa. While the mother was speaking with Gerontissa, Sr. Agapia was holding the baby, and she was speaking to him the way we all do when we get to hold little bundles of joy. The baby was only a few months old, and Sr. Agapia asked him, "Will you walk with Jesus all the days of your life?"

And to Sr. Agapia's utter amazement, the baby said, "Yes, I will."

Completely stunned that she just heard the infant speak, she ran to Gerontissa.

"Gerontissa, I just asked the baby if he was going to live for Jesus and he spoke and said he would!"

In Gerontissa's characteristic nonchalant manner, she said, "It's true, he will."

At the baptism of another baby boy, the child fell asleep shortly after the service ended, as many babies do after being baptized, and his two hands were distinctly held in the form of the Orthodox blessing: ICXC. These Greek letters are spelled by the positioning of the fingers and are the first and last letters in the Greek words *Iesous* and *Xristos* (Jesus Christ). In keeping with tradition, the priest gives the blessing with his right hand and the placement of his fingers forms these initials. Bishops give this blessing with both hands. Perhaps one day that child will be called *Despota.* *

During the baptism of an adult, after she came up from the water on the third immersion, she looked at the priest and said, "Why did you pull me out of there? I wanted to stay there." She had seen something while she was in the water, but she did not reveal to anyone in attendance what exactly she experienced.

When Gerontissa Philareti was four months old, she was baptized in the family's parish church in her village. Her mother's sister was her godmother, and during the service when the priest handed the godmother the child's lit candle—which the godparent holds on behalf of the child—Gerontissa reached out and held it herself. Even as a tiny infant she held the large candle all by herself while the priest led the party around the font, chanting, "As many of ye as were baptized into Christ."

Afterwards the priest told them, "That is a sign that she will bring much light to many people." And that is exactly what she grew up to do!

Pure Beeswax Candles

ONE BRIGHT WEEK, WE WENT out to visit the nuns and help them with the upcoming feast of St. George. (In Greece, whenever St. George's feast day falls during Great Lent or close to Pascha, it is moved to Bright Week.) The monastery's neighboring village has a great devotion to St. George the Great Martyr, so the monastery often gets at least a few hundred pilgrims. They set up tents with sweets and coffee and some of the monastery's products. They also put out about five large metal candle boxes filled with sand for the people to light candles outside the church.

On this particular day, I stayed with Sr. Sarah selling the monastery's canned and baked goods while John was with Sr. Lydia's grandfather, Mr. George, tending to the hundreds of lit candles.

Mr. George was passionate about candles as representing our prayer offerings to God. And so it was with a good—if funny—disposition that he struggled with the thought that some pilgrims chose to light paraffin candles. Since he and John were in charge of snuffing out the candles once they burned low enough, he took great delight in putting out the paraffin ones. He would shake his head and comment to himself (albeit aloud), *"Parafini!"*

At one point, he gestured to some pure beeswax candles and said to John, "Now these, *these* are pure offerings to God!"

John and I found Mr. George's disdain for paraffin candles amusing, but in Mr. George's defense, Elder Paisios the Athonite had shared a similar thought about offering pure beeswax candles to God.

KNOT SIXTEEN

In a conversation with someone, the elder explained how man takes so much from God and yet gives so little in return:

We eat sweet fruit and offer the resin of trees to God with the censer. We eat honey and we offer the wax to God, but even this we mix with paraffin. We offer one candle to God out of gratitude for His many blessings and even this we adulterate! ... It is possible for someone to practice economy in everything, except in the worship of God. One should give the purest and best things to God. ... Does God have need of these things? No! But God helps because He sees the pure heart, the good disposition; in this way the good intention is expressed.[11]

17

KNOT SEVENTEEN

The Hermitage of St. Theodora

A SMALL, OLD CHAPEL IS LOCATED in the woods about a forty-five-minute walk from the monastery. It is named after St. Theodora of Thessaloniki. She lived in the ninth century and was originally from Aegina, but fled with her husband and child when Muslims took over the island.

It was not long after they settled in Thessaloniki that her husband died. St. Theodora, having already entrusted their daughter to a monastery, joined her child in the monastic life. She often heard angels singing, and after a long and righteous life, died in the year 879.

In earlier times, this chapel served as the common church for the surrounding hermits. Archaeologists say hermits lived in that area as early as the thirteenth century. Whether the contemporary chapel was originally the cell of a hermit is disputed, but to me it didn't look like it was ever meant to be anything other than a chapel. Today this little chapel is the only visible remains of the old hermitage* that once existed. A holy spring pours out into a very small pool, the source of which is somewhere in the chapel's foundation. An icon of St. Theodora hangs just above the streaming spring; a metal cup attached to a chain hangs on a nail just underneath it. This is the common cup from which pilgrims drink when they visit the hermitage.

This small church was built right in the side of a hill with a rather large grassy area in front of it. I have gone there many times. The path is well worn, if a little difficult; but it is also very holy.

In the fourteenth century a well-known and beloved Greek saint walked that same path to visit his spiritual father, who lived at a hermitage in the area. With the blessing of his spiritual father, this saint later founded a monastery on an island in Greece and was martyred by Turks there.

Many, many, years later—when God saw fit—the saint revealed himself to a nun and directed her to find his relics. He finally became a "known" saint. Many people throughout the world have a great devotion to him due to his many miracles, which reveal his love for struggling Christians. It was an honor to walk the same path he trod.

Once, a group of us decided to go to the chapel. We asked Gerontissa for her blessing, and on receiving it, we headed out in the direction of the little church. The nuns gave us oil to fill the lamps, new wicks to place inside them, a lighter to light them, and a bottle to fill up with water from the holy spring, which they give out in small bottles to pilgrims who visit the monastery.

The chapel was rather dark with the door closed since it only had one small west-facing window. It had a small iconostasis with three icons—Christ, Panagia, and St. Theodora. The floor was originally dirt, but it was later covered with slabs of rock.

Since there were six of us and we were in no hurry, we replenished the oil lamps, lit them, swept, lit some candles, and opened one of the service books to sing a part of the supplication service to the saint. The two girls from Athens mostly sang it, since John and I and the other couple with us only know Greek as a second language and don't read ancient Greek very quickly. So we just stuck to the responses: "O holy saint of God, pray to God for us," "Most Holy Theotokos, save us," and, "Glory to the Father, and to the Son, and to the Holy Spirit."

Afterward we went outside to the spring. We each took turns drinking from it using the metal cup. We sat on the nearby benches—made of tree trunks—and spoke a little before we began our return trek.

I told the others that Sr. Theologia had informed me that none of the relics of the hermits had ever been found. But once, when a group of pilgrims visited the hermitage, two women, sitting on the very benches we were sitting on, heard a knocking noise coming from the earth. They didn't know what to do, so they informed the sisterhood of the strange noise, and the sisters took it as a sign that perhaps an unknown saint rests there. I suppose only time will tell if God sees fit to reveal any of the God-fearing saints who most certainly struggled and died in that area.

On our way back, having taken a detour toward an open field and having become a bit confused as to where we should go, we went down a small hill with bushes to get into the clearing. While walking down the hill, suddenly I saw a long bright green thing quickly squirm through the long grass away from me to my left. I screamed like a girl in a horror film and stood frozen as I watched another one to my right run in the opposite direction. Then I realized they were lizards, not snakes.

Thank God! I breathed a sigh of relief.

Although I quickly got myself out of the long grass and into the field, I managed to see that the lizards were bright green with bright blue bellies. They were about two feet long, head to tail. It makes for an interesting story but not such a pleasant experience. Although I didn't do what the nuns told us to do if we saw a snake (make the sign of the cross over it), I'm relieved I only screamed and didn't say any bad words.

On returning to the monastery, I told the nuns what I had seen, and they said once one of those lizards got into the sisters' cells. While one nun was trying to trap it, the other nuns started coming out of their cells to see what all the ruckus was. When they saw the lizard, a good bit of screaming ensued, but fortunately they were able to capture it.

Working for the Glory of God and an Interesting Story

EVERY EVENING, ONE OF THE NUNS waters all the flowers in the monastery. Throughout the monastery were terracotta pots shaped in forms reminiscent of the old pots Greeks used to keep olive oil in years ago—rather tall with a base smaller than the top, with handles on each side. It seemed as though there was always a plethora of flowers overflowing from each one.

One evening while I was walking through the courtyard, I saw Sr. Agathi standing on the benches watering the flowers on the ledge above. She greeted me, so I stopped to chat with her, and somehow we got into the following conversation.

"Gerontissa Philareti always told us, whatever we do, whether it's watering flowers, baking, cleaning, cooking, whatever, not to do it for ourselves, not for the sisterhood, and not even for Gerontissa, but to do it for God alone.

"If we do it for any other reason or for any other person, we can become disappointed or embittered. We can have stupid thoughts that tell us *so-and-so doesn't appreciate what I do for them*, and so on. But when we do our work solely for God, we do not look for recognition or gratitude; we do it out of love and don't expect to get anything in return. Even if we do receive a reward, we don't know what it will be or even when it will be. So we continue working for Him; if it earns us rewards, then may God see fit to grant them to us. But in any case, whatever we do, we should do it for Him."

This reminds me of something the twins once shared with me. Sr. Monica and Sr. Margaret started visiting the monastery when they were children, as many from the sisterhood did. They told me that when they were young, Gerontissa told them whenever someone does something to help a monastery, God repays that person immediately (whether or not he or she notices this).

"Any work we do in a monastery is solely done in honor of the saint and God, no matter how small it is. Even if it's only picking up a small piece of garbage, we gain a fortune from it," Gerontissa had said.

At this point Sr. Marina joined in the twins' story by saying, "And so when we were young we used to run around the monastery searching for garbage we could pick up!"

Hearing this, the four of us laughed, but this simple anecdote stayed with me.

Afterward, whenever I was working at the monastery, I would recall this story and while folding boxes or cleaning jars, drying dishes or stocking the bookstore, I would pray for my deceased relatives by saying, "Lord Jesus Christ, have mercy on your servant." And I would say to the patron saint of the monastery, "Let this work be as alms for their souls since I don't have much money to give away."

The nuns always told me that although we do not write down

non-Orthodox names for commemoration in the church, there are other ways to pray for these people. That is, since we neither give their names for the *proskomidi*,* nor for supplication services or memorials, the best way to help non-Orthodox who have departed is by saying the Jesus Prayer for them and giving alms in their name. I hope that my deceased relatives have at least benefited from my small amount of alms, since my prayers are weak and few and far between.

This story, of course, reminds me of another story I was told by my pious professor of dogmatic theology at Aristotle University of Thessaloniki.

He told us about a priest he knew from Thessaloniki who once, while serving the Proskomidi, was cutting the crumbs for the souls of the living. As he was placing the crumbs onto the *diskos*,* one crumb fell to the ground. He picked it up and placed it back on the diskos, but again it fell off. He repeated this once more, but when it fell off the third time, he understood this to be a sign indicating something was wrong. So he took the small piece of paper with the names on it that he had just read, opened the north door of the iconostasis, and said to the women, "Who wrote the names on this paper?"

After the woman was discovered, he asked to speak with her.

"This name here, who is it?" he asked.

"It's the husband of a relative of mine," she explained.

"Is he Orthodox?"

"Well, no . . . but since he is married to an Orthodox Christian I thought I could write his name down."

"Don't do that again," the priest instructed her. "The Church only permits us to pray for non-Orthodox privately."

18

KNOT EIGHTEEN

In the Porch Preparing the Candles

ON THE RIGHT SIDE of the monastery's large church is a small outer porch. Quite a few churches and monasteries in Greece have them. They are outside of the church but have a roof and often have benches along the sides. They function as a sort of outer narthex. Archeologists say that the outer porch at this monastery used to be covered in frescoes. Today you can still see small portions of icons of the Judgment and a depiction of some scenes from the Book of Revelation, but that is all.

One summer evening, Sisters Akakia and Agathi were sitting on the benches in the porch preparing the candles and asked me to help them. There were piles of dark, pure beeswax candles wrapped in bundles of ten. These candles were going to be put in all the chandeliers in the church. This is how churches used to be lit everywhere. Unfortunately, these days most churches have switched to electric lights. Of course, it's more practical, but less peaceful.

I remember hearing a wonderful homily by a priest in Greece, Fr. Andreas Kanonas, in which he said the reason monastery churches are so dark, lit only by oil lamps and candles, is to encourage watchfulness. I found that rather interesting because I used to think going into a dark church in the middle of the night for a vigil would make you feel more sleepy. However, Fr. Andreas pointed out that when one is in the dark, the human eye naturally opens wider in order to see. This, of course, can be confirmed by anyone who has ever gotten up in the night. On returning from the bathroom or kitchen (if the light was on), notice how automatically your eyes open wide, struggling to see as best you can. This is the same effect a dimly lit church has on the faithful: The eyes open wide, straining to see, and in this way the soul is also awakened to watchfulness.

Srs. Akakia and Agathi were each holding seven candles together. They would light the seven candles with a small beeswax candle, the bottom of which they stuck onto the stone bench so that it continued to burn until the next time they needed it. Having lit the candles, they waited for the wicks to burn down until the tip of the candle's wax started melting. Then they would take a folded piece of packaging paper and pinch the flame out. They did this because during the services, the candles are lit after they have been placed in the hanging chandeliers; burning the wicks beforehand helps them take fire more readily.

They let me start with five candles, but when Sr. Agathi saw I was being cowardly and nervous around the fire, she gave me a skeptical look and asked, "Can you do it?"

"Yes," I said. "I'm just a bit nervous around fire at first. I'll catch on, though." She continued to watch me while I tried jerkily to light all the candles and snuff them, afraid the heat from the small flames would burn me.

"Give them to me," Sr. Agathi said. "You can do three at a time instead."

Once I got the hang of it, I tried to move my way back up to five, but Sr. Agathi didn't let me.

Sr. Akakia and Sr. Agathi are first cousins, but you would never know it. Their personalities are as different as their outward appearances; I could hardly believe they were related. They are both very sweet, but Sr. Agathi is a big tormentor and always had great fun teasing me. Sr. Akakia, on the other hand, was very quiet, but was amused easily and had a wonderfully contagious laugh.

While we were burning the candle wicks, they asked me how John and I became Orthodox. I told them a few details of what we were like before we found Orthodoxy and how my family became Orthodox. That is how the following conversation came about.

Sr. Akakia's older brother was the first to start looking into the Church. He had been having a hard time, so he decided to go to a nearby church to see if he could speak with the priest. By the grace of God, he found him just as he was exiting the church's side door. After this encounter with the priest, her brother changed. He confessed for the first time and started living a spiritual life. Naturally, he spoke about the Church and life in Christ to his sister and in turn, their cousin, Sr. Agathi. Gradually the girls also started living spiritual lives, attending church services, confessing and communing on a regular basis. In the end they decided to become nuns, and he became a hieromonk.

When we were alone, Sr. Agathi told me something she experienced during the period when she was rediscovering Orthodoxy. One evening after she finished the Compline service, she was feeling rather overwhelmed by her sins and passions, and with tears she prayed to the Lord, "My God, why did You not make me an angel when You created me? If I were an angel I would be able to praise and glorify You unceasingly. But as it is, my sins and passions overcome my resolve to live for You."

Finishing her plea, Sr. Agathi heard a voice: "But if I had made you an angel, you might have been among those that fell."

She was completely taken aback by this unfamiliar voice, but knew in her heart it was from God, and for the first time she understood the great importance of repentance. Because of repentance, no matter what we've done, we always have the hope of salvation through the great mercy of the forgiving Lord. The fallen angels, however, will never repent, since an angel's choice is made once and made forever.

Monastery Tea: A Gift from the Saint

DURING THE SUMMER MONTHS, the nuns gather tea leaves from the trees and mountainsides surrounding the monastery. They lay them out to dry, then bag and sell them in the bookstore. They have mountain tea (a Greek favorite), lavender tea, black tea, and linden tea.

During the summer nights, with the stars shining brightly above us, we would set up tables in the courtyard, pull up chairs, and turn on the outside lights. Taking handfuls of dried tea leaves, we placed them in small plastic bags and handed them to the two sisters whose task it was to seal them. The nice, warm breeze was a welcome refreshment from the humid summer days. Seeing the bags stuffed with tea leaves, I asked Sr. Irene, "How much do you sell these for, four or five euros?"

"No!" she said laughing. "That's expensive! We sell them for *one* euro. You know these tea leaves are a gift from the saint. He allows them to grow so we can make some money to support ourselves. They are a pure blessing; we don't have to do any work to cultivate them. We just pick the leaves; *the saint* does all the work."

I loved their tea. It was a comfort and a blessing to drink it. Sr. Euphemia was a pro at making tea. Any problem you had, she'd make you some tea and it would take care of your ailment. If you had a headache, she'd make you a cup of chamomile. If your stomach was upset, she'd make you peppermint or oregano tea (which tasted wretched, but really did help). On cold winter days she'd make you mountain tea for breakfast. If you felt really ill, she'd make you what she called her "super tea," combining different leaves. You'd laugh when you heard her say "super" with a Greek accent, but appreciate it when her "super tea" alleviated your aches and pains.

One evening John and I were sitting with some friends in the reception area, and Sr. Nektaria sat down to speak with us. We were talking about her work in the garden, and she said, "Tomorrow I'm getting up early because the workers and I are going for tea in the mountains before work in the garden starts."

"What time are you going?" I asked.

"Around six."

"*Before* you go to the garden to do all your work?"

"Yes," she said.

"How often do you go to the mountain for tea with Mr. John and Mr. Theodore?" I asked, thinking she was crazy for getting up so early to drink tea in the mountains with the workers.

"Whenever we need to pick it," she answered.

"Oh my goodness, Nektaria!" I said, laughing. "I thought you meant you were going to the mountain to *drink* tea!" At this we all busted up laughing.

"Gerontissa! Constantina thought I was going to the mountain to drink tea with Mr. John and Mr. Theodore tomorrow morning!" Sr. Nektaria reported.

Gerontissa, who had just come in to sit down with us, started laughing. "A picnic!" she said, in her thick Greek accent.

Eldress Macrina of Volos

ONE EVENING A HANDFUL OF US were in the church washing floors and wiping down chairs and stasidia in preparation for a feast day. While we were washing the floors, I noticed poor Sr. Theologia was so tired that even though she was standing up and mopping, her eyes kept closing, and it was clear she was falling asleep. She managed to finish her work, and I teased her about being the only person I knew who could sleep and mop at the same time. She just laughed.

While we cleaned the church, Sr. Akakia and I started having a conversation about a well-known abbess from Volos. Sr. Akakia had read some things about her and had heard some stories. She told me that Eldress Macrina was born in 1921 in Smyrna but was left an orphan around the young age of ten. Before her parents died, however, she received their blessing to become a nun when she grew older. She did indeed become a nun, in the Holy Monastery of Panagia Odigitria (the Directress) in Portaria, Volos, under the spiritual guidance of Elder Joseph the Hesychast (+1959).

Until that time, however, she was left on the streets to raise her younger brother. In the beginning, people would offer them food. But later, during the war, things were so difficult that no one paid attention to the young orphans. By the providence of God, she first found work crushing walnuts for a little bread, and later she worked in a tobacco factory.

Sr. Akakia told me the eldress's job consisted of counting the cigarettes and placing twenty-five of them in each cigarette package. Having her mind occupied with counting cigarettes bothered her because it distracted her from being able to pray with a fully attentive mind. So one day, with great faith and simplicity, she said to the Mother of God, "Panagia, I am not able to both pray and count these cigarettes; so I will pray and you will count them."

After that she no longer concerned herself with how many cigarettes she placed in the package, because she had faith that the Mother of God would grant her request. The eldress prayed and, as it turned out, the Mother of God counted the cigarettes for her, because there were always twenty-five in a package.

Another story Sr. Akakia told me about Eldress Macrina took place in the monastery when she was the abbess. One evening she came out of her cell and into the hall and saw a woman wearing a blue blouse and a blue skirt with her long hair undone, walking down the corridor. She assumed it was one of the nuns doing her prayer rule in her pajamas (nuns usually wear their pajamas under their rasso) with her hair unbraided.

The next day the eldress addressed the sisterhood: "Who was doing their prayer rule in the hallway last night?"

Each of the nuns said it was not her. That night the abbess saw the same woman again. She asked the sisterhood about her again, and again they said it was not one of them. The next evening, once more, she saw the woman in the corridor and sure enough, when she asked the sisterhood about it the next day, each one said it wasn't her.

KNOT EIGHTEEN

Once Eldress Macrina noticed that the sisterhood was starting to draw the conclusion that she was seeing someone *else*, she stopped asking them about it.

"It was Panagia, Constantina," Sr. Akakia told me, smiling.

Eldress Macrina was called a second Tabitha, "full of good works" (Acts 9:36), who helped countless people—not only in Volos, but throughout Greece. In 1995 she fell asleep in the Lord, but no doubt remains an intercessor for those who seek her help and prayers. There is a booklet about her in Greek and a book being prepared for publication. I am hopeful that someday we will have this book in English. It is filled with her simple but profound wisdom—sayings such as, "We will have pain and affliction because without these we cannot reach the heavens."

I believe we have much to learn from such a great contemporary female saint who, after suffering much, received much. For "we also glory in tribulations, knowing that tribulation produces perseverance; and perseverance, character; and character, hope. Now hope does not disappoint" (Rom. 5:3–5).

KNOT NINETEEN

Blaming Oneself

ONE SATURDAY AFTERNOON MY HUSBAND and I were helping in the bookstore. While we were taking jars of pickled vegetables out of the refrigerator to label and place them on the shelves, we noticed some mold had grown on the surface of the liquid. Seeing this, Sr. Seraphima sighed. She began opening the handful of jars in order to clean out the mold.

In a monastery nothing goes to waste. So once the mold was removed, the jars were set aside to be carted over to the kitchen so that the pickled vegetables could be eaten by the sisters.

"It's because of my sins. God allowed this to happen because of my sins," Sr. Seraphima reflected while cleaning out the mold.

Both my husband's and my first thought was, *What sins?* Since neither one of us could imagine that Sr. Seraphima, who had been an extremely pious nun from a young age—for over twenty years—would have great sins to be punished for. But regardless of how big or small her personal sins were, we saw the benefit of this way of thinking.

Blaming ourselves when we play some role in things going wrong, or even when unfortunate things happen beyond our control, is a strategic preemptive strike against our ego and our passions. In each instance, if we blame ourselves first, we will come out the victor. This is not a morbid attempt at self-abuse, but a clever means of keeping in check one's temper, self-righteousness, criticism of others, and grumbling against God. If we always blame ourselves, we will accept our circumstances with a humble heart.

Sr. Seraphima set a very good example for us in modeling herself after our forefather Job the long-suffering. Job never once grumbled but blessed God; he willingly and humbly accepted his circumstances. To see her accept this small misfortune with such a spiritual outlook made a lasting impact on us.

Eating with Greeks

THROUGHOUT MY VISITS to the monastery, I witnessed many interesting comments and events during mealtimes, with visitors and nuns alike. The following stories provide a glimpse into what it means to eat with (or in the presence of) Greeks.

One afternoon Mrs. Dina and I were eating fish together for lunch. As I mentioned before, the nuns often baked and served the entire body, including the head, of the fish. Thus, I was struggling a little at the beginning trying to eat the fish while avoiding all the bones. Mrs. Dina kept watching me all the while with concern. By this point she had finished her meal, and seeing that I was still struggling, she said, "Would you like me to clean your fish for you? I just washed my hands."

Accepting defeat, I handed her my plate. I was not going to manage to eat all that fish meat if I had to stop every few seconds to dig out a bone. She took a knife and cut the fish in two from the underside of the tail to the head and started taking out all the bones. She put all the bones to one side and the fish meat to the other.

"There," she said, "try eating it now."

After some time she asked, "Aren't you going to eat the head?"

"No," I said hesitantly.

"Oh, we eat the heads. They're good for you."

"Well, we don't. You want it?"

"Sure," she said, taking it.

Eating with Mrs. Dina was like eating with my grandmother. She took care of me as if I were a child needing to be fed.

Something I noticed about many Greeks is that they can't understand how you can eat a meal without bread. Every time I ate with Mrs. Dina, she would pass me the bread basket and tell me to take some. At first I refused, not feeling the need to eat bread when the nuns had put so much food on my plate. But after seeing her become grieved enough times when I refused, and after hearing her say, "You need to eat bread, it's good for you," too many times, I just started taking a slice each time she offered it to me. Then when she wasn't looking, I'd put them back in the basket!

A lot of the Greeks I ate with also found that I ate very little. I remember visiting the monastery once with my godmother and eating lunch with a group of women. When someone offered me seconds, I politely refused, and to my surprise one of the women (whom I didn't remember, though she looked familiar) said, "Oh, no, she doesn't eat very much. I've eaten with her before and noticed that."

I found that rather peculiar, but I guess some people notice those things and think a "growing young woman" needs to eat more. (To tell the truth, I avoided stuffing myself full of vegetables and bread so I could save room for sweets! But that bad habit seemed to go unnoticed—at least at *that* time it did.)

Whenever we ate with Mrs. Maria (Sr. Silouani's sister) she, like most Greek women, would force me to eat more. Whenever I asked her to pass me the water, she would comment while pouring, "You drink a lot of water when you eat! But it *is* blessed water, very blessed water."

This always made my husband laugh.

One lunchtime I came into the dining hall where Elder Isidoros the blind was already eating. Sr. Raphaela was attending to him. She pointed to a seat and quietly said, "That's your place, Constantina. Marina gave you a chocolate donut because she knows you like chocolate. Isn't that right?"

"Yes," I said.

The elder overheard this and said, "We shouldn't eat what we *like*, but what we *need*. Constantina, what kind of food do you dislike?"

"White rice. We ate it too often when we lived in Asia and now I don't really like it."

"Which do you like better, rice or Fr. Luke?" he asked, referring to my spiritual father, whom he had met when Fr. Luke visited Philotheou Monastery. At this Sr. Raphaela and I exchanged looks with big smiles.

"I like Fr. Luke better," I answered.

"Well, from now on call rice 'Luke,' and eat it!" the elder said, in his characteristically entertaining manner.

"May it be blessed," I said, laughing.

One evening, Mrs. Maria and I were eating dinner together when Sr. Silouani came in. She stopped to talk to us and said to me, "Constandia [that's how she always pronounced my name], you've gained weight!"

"I know I gained a little here," I said, tapping my stomach.

"No, not there. Here!" Sr. Silouani said, indicating my backside.

I started laughing. "Sister!" I said.

But that wasn't the only comment about my weight that trip.

The next day at lunch Mrs. Maria and I each had our own salad. I had eaten everything on my main plate and tried a piece of eggplant the nuns had prepared as a side dish, so I had no room left to eat my salad.

This upset Mrs. Maria and she said, "Eat! Eat your salad!"

"I'm too full," I confessed.

When Sr. Savina came out of the nun's dining hall, Mrs. Maria told her, "Look, Sister! Constantina didn't eat her salad."

I have no idea what made her say that, but boy did I ever hear it from Sr. Savina!

(Sr. Savina was one of the older nuns. I had been visiting the monastery for two and a half years at the point this story took place, and she had spoken to me maybe twice.)

"Constantina, why didn't you eat your salad? You don't like salad?" she asked.

"Salad is my favorite, but I'm too full," I said.

"Yeah, you're too full because you eat too many sweets!" she responded. I just looked at her wide-eyed.

"Do you know how you have become?" she said, getting louder. "Like this!" she said, putting her hands behind her back to indicate a large backside.

Utterly taken by surprise, but finding her too funny to keep a straight face, I burst out laughing.

"Well, by your prayers I'll try not to eat so many sweets," I said, still laughing. Once she had spoken her mind, she turned and slowly walked away.

When I told the nuns what Sr. Savina said, I couldn't stop laughing.

They just shook their heads. "Savina! Don't pay any attention to her, Constantina. She says stuff like that to everyone."

"Take it for humility," Sr. Xenia suggested.

"That was one of very few times Sr. Savina has ever spoken to me! Maybe she thinks I have hope of improvement since she bothered to speak to me," I said, trying to make light of her criticism. The sisters just responded with smiles.

A few days later I saw Sr. Savina again and told her, "Sister, I'd just like you to know that since you spoke to me the other day, I haven't eaten any sweets."

"Yeah, well, when you go home you're going to be throwing them in your mouth!" she said with a flat expression, putting her hand to her mouth to indicate just how I would "throw" them.

"No, Sister, by your prayers I'll try not to," I said, smiling, but trying to take her seriously.

"Excuse me for what I said, it's just you're very tall and it's a shame if you become fat," she calmly explained.

"I understand. Thank you, by your prayers I'll try harder," I said.

And I did try harder—for a few weeks.

The next day when I was preparing to leave, Sr. Lydia packed a lot of food for me to take home, but I refused a lot of it. So she went to the abbess: "Gerontissa, Constantina doesn't want to take any food with her because Savina called her fat," she said.

"That's not why!" I said, laughing.

"Constantina, don't pay any attention to Savina," Gerontissa said, smiling.

"No, really I just thought it was too much food to take," I said.

In the end I yielded. "May it be blessed!"

20

KNOT TWENTY

Thy Priests, O Lord, Shall Be Clothed with Righteousness

MANY PRIESTS THAT SERVE the Divine Liturgy at the monastery are very pious, holy priests. Here are some of their stories.

Fr. Andrew was probably the priest who liturgized most frequently at the monastery. He is from an island in southern Greece. Even as a young man, he knew he wanted to become a priest. However, in order to become a clergyman, a man needs to be married before ordination (unless he is a monk). So Fr. Andrew went to an orphanage run by nuns and said, "I want to become a priest, and so I need a good, pious girl to marry. Can you suggest one for me from the orphanage?"

The nuns chose one of the most pious girls in the orphanage. The two married and now live in a village near the monastery with their four children. He became a good priest and fasts strictly, often to the point of fatigue. His wife, aided by the fact that she was raised by nuns, became an ideal presvytera.*

After serving some time at a parish, Fr. Andrew was raised to the level of archpriest and brought to the cathedral to serve near the bishop. His wife, in order to help him remain humble, would often tell him, "Take off that gold cross! Do you think you are someone special because you serve with the bishop? Just because you serve in the cathedral doesn't make you a good priest. A good priest has humility!"

He took it all very well, with a grateful heart, often telling the nuns, "I have a *good* presvytera; she humbles me."

The teenaged daughter of another priest who occasionally served at the monastery was diagnosed with cancer. While she was in the hospital overnight, awaiting surgery in the morning, she had a dream in which an old doctor with white hair and a white beard operated on her. The dream left such a strong impact on her that she felt as if she had actually experienced it.

The next morning, when the doctors came in to operate on her, they saw that the cancer was nowhere to be found. They did not proceed with the scheduled operation.

Once the young woman returned home, she explained to her mother what she had seen in her dream. Her mother started showing her different icons of various saints, trying to find out the identity of the mysterious doctor. Finally, the teenager saw a photograph of St. Luke of Crimea which her mother had in her wallet.

"That was him! That's the doctor who operated on me!" she exclaimed in amazement.

This is how the family learned that it was St. Luke the Physician, Bishop of Crimea and new martyr, who had operated on their daughter and cured her of cancer.

A visiting hieromonk from America once liturgized for the nuns. After he left the altar, Sr. Akakia, acting as ecclesiarch, went into the sanctuary to tidy up. She was struck by a potent aroma, and perceiving that it was a result of the Divine Liturgy served by the hieromonk, she said to the sisters, "Come and smell the sanctuary. It's fragrant!"

Sr. Euphemia told me many priests who liturgize at the monastery were accompanied by fragrance while serving at the altar. She said many times when she went into the altar to get the censer, she was taken aback by the potency of the aroma in the altar. "Sometimes it's so strong it's like stepping into a room full of burning incense."

Another hieromonk, who was a childhood companion of Gerontissa, once told the nuns how important it is for us not to become comfortable or over familiar in sacred places. His spiritual father had told him, "Never let the space where you stand in front of the altar become ordinary." He went on to explain that carelessness creeps in when we relate to sacred things and sacred places with complacency.

One spring evening, Gerontissa Philareti was speaking to my husband and me about the sacredness of the holy priesthood and the great responsibility that accompanies it.

"The holy priesthood is an office," she told us. "The priest will go before God at the Judgment with a great amount of responsibility because he is in charge of many souls, and this is why it is very difficult for a priest to be saved. He must be very, *very* careful; he can't even speak a harsh word to someone, because then how will he liturgize?

"The priesthood is not something one should rush into. Everything in the spiritual life requires time. We should never rush in our spiritual life. We have a saying, *If you rush, you will trip.*

"And you should know that if the presvytera is good, the priest will be good. Behind every good married priest is a good presvytera," she said, looking at me.

"*You* have to be perfect," she added.

"What do you mean, Gerontissa? What do I have to do?" I asked nervously.

"Just keep doing what you're doing. Obey your spiritual father, confess thoroughly, and commune as often as you can. Don't judge, don't criticize—not even in your thoughts. You have to pray the Jesus Prayer a lot, be vigilant, and you must show a lot of respect to John when he is a priest."

"Once you are ordained, John, temptations will come. My good friend Fr. Chrysostomos used to say, 'It's like there is an 'x' with a circle around it on the newly ordained priest's chest. Temptations continually hit the target.'"

To further illustrate the sacredness of the priesthood, she told us, "Yesterday a priest visited and spoke with me in private. He told me that at a Divine Liturgy he was serving recently, while lifting the bread and wine up and saying, '*Ta sa ek ton soon*' (Thine own of Thine own), his hands suddenly filled with the sacred Blood of Christ. He was just standing there, shocked, with his hands full of blood, not knowing what to do.

"He immediately thought: '*If this doesn't go away, how will I be able to go out and commune the people?*'

"He prayed for the Lord to take it away, and He did."

She did not explain any of this to us. She neither told us the reason she shared the story, nor offered an opinion on why the priest experienced that miraculous event. But regardless, it most definitely made an impression on us: Holy things are for the holy.

KNOT TWENTY

Preparing the Prozimi

MIRACULOUS *PROZIMI** is a special ingredient in traditional prosphora, which is the bread that becomes Christ's Body in the Divine
Liturgy. It is the only rising agent the sisters put into their recipe.
Unfortunately, it is no longer a main ingredient in the prosphora used
in most churches today. This is obvious because prozimi produces a
sourdough taste. So, once you've tasted it, you can always identify
prosphora that has prozimi in it.

How prozimi is made is a miracle of the Orthodox Church, but not
a very well-known one. It can only happen twice a year: on the Feast of
the Precious and Life-Giving Cross, September 14, and during the reading of the Epistle during the Vesperal Divine Liturgy of Holy Thursday.

One winter evening, with the warm wood stove burning, I joined
Sr. Sarah and Sr. Thekla in the bakery to see how they prepare the
prozimi. They had already placed the water on the stove to heat it up.
Once the water was the right temperature, they added the flour and a
small portion of prozimi. After this they started kneading.

They asked me if I was "clean," and they told me that they only
make prosphora when they do not have their menstrual cycle. I started
kneading the mixture, and they told me, "Say the *Most Holy Theotokos
save me* prayer and the *Rejoice, Theotokos and Virgin.*"

While I kneaded and prayed, they told me the miracle surrounding
the prozimi: "On the feast of the Precious and Life-Giving Cross, we
put a bowl of water and flour in the altar, and the priest blesses it with
a branch of basil in the sign of the cross. Gerontissa then stirs it and
leaves it for a day. By the grace of God, through the priest's blessing,
the mixture rises as though it were regular yeast.

"If we want more prozimi, we can do the same thing again during the Vesperal Divine Liturgy on Holy Thursday morning. While the Epistle is being read, when the Reader says, 'Take eat; this is my body' (1 Cor. 11:24), Gerontissa stirs the mixture. Once left for the night it too will rise as though it were yeast," Sr. Thekla explained.

Afterward, this mixture is kept in airtight containers in a freezer for the rest of the year. Each time the nuns prepare the prozimi, before baking the prosphora, they set aside a small amount in a container and use it in the next batch. This way the prozimi lasts all year. As a blessing, the nuns even use a little bit of it in their regular bread.

"Now we will place this mixture in pots," Sr. Thekla continued, "and wrap the pots in garbage bags and blankets to keep the mixture warm, allowing it to rise. Early tomorrow morning we will unwrap the blankets and take off the garbage bags, we'll see how high the prozimi has risen, and then we'll use it as our sole source of yeast in all the prosphora. While making them we pray the Akathist Hymn to Panagia.

"Constantina, you should get the recipe from Sr. Irene and make prosphora at home. We can give you some prozimi to keep in your refrigerator, and you can get a prosphora seal from the bookstore. They're made on the Holy Mountain," Sr. Thekla said.

A Greek-style prosphora seal is a circular wooden stamp that contains five squares. The only ones I have ever seen are hand-carved. The nuns always said the nicest ones come from the monks on Mount Athos, since they carve the design quite deeply, which produces a more pronounced print on the bread.

The three squares running vertically through the center are called lambs because those sections of the bread become the Body of Christ. Each has the imprint IC XC and NI KA (Jesus Christ Conquers). The center square is used as the Body of Christ every Divine Liturgy, while one of the other two is scraped with a knife from the underside, allowing the crumbs to fall onto the diskos while the priest commemorates both living and dead Orthodox Christians.

The square on the right side of the seal has a triangular shape within it, called the *Panagia* because it is placed on the altar next to the piece called the lamb—representing the Panagia herself, who stood next to the Lamb of God while He hung on the Tree.

The square on the left-hand side has nine small triangles within it, which represent the nine ranks of angels. Together, the three lambs, the Panagia, and the nine ranks of angels form the sign of the cross.

I had never heard of the miracle of prozimi, nor the significance of the prosphora seal before meeting the sisters. There are so many miracles—so much wealth—in the Orthodox Church, and so few of us hear of them!

On Good Works

THE SISTERHOOD HAD COME UPON some problem that required the rental of some large freezers for a few years, so they looked into some places that rent such utilities. A sister called one of the companies to inquire about the availability of two freezers and to ask the rental price. The woman on the line said the typical price to rent one of their freezers was around three thousand euros a month, but since it was for a monastery she would check with the owner to see if they could offer a discount.

A few days later the woman returned the nun's call to tell her the owner's decision. As it turned out, the owner had the same name as the patron saint of the monastery. When he heard the monastery of his namesake was in need, he was more than willing to help. He said,

"I feel as though the saint wants me to lend the monastery our utilities for free."

So the woman told the sister on the line, "He said he will lend you two freezers and one refrigerator free of charge for as long as you need them. Whenever you need them, just call and we will have them delivered."

Truly God takes care of us in all situations!

Whether this man was a churchgoer or not is of little significance; it would not in the least surprise me if he were not. Even in many non-churchgoing Greeks you can still see a faith that runs deep. Regardless of this man's standing with the Church, he allowed himself to be moved by the grace of God through His saint, and he will certainly reap the benefits of his charity.

A similar good work was done by a woman from the nearby village. In order to repair the nuns' living quarters, the sisterhood wanted to take out a bank loan. But since the amount was great, and they had no means to show they could pay it back, their request was rejected.

A pious woman who owns a factory went to the bank and took out the loan in her own name so that the monastery could receive the funds they needed. They would merely give her the minimum payment each month so she could pay it to the bank.

Following her offer to supply the monastery with the bank loan, Gerontissa told the sisters that by offering this kind of alms the woman was building a palace for herself in Paradise.

"When she dies, she will be considered a *builder* of the monastery!" Gerontissa assured them.

The mother of one of the nuns did a comparable sacrificial good work when she allowed her daughter to become a nun before she was of the age legally permitted to make such a decision.

KNOT TWENTY

When this nun was young, she really wanted to become a monastic, but her mother was hesitant to let her go. After a long time her mother finally agreed to allow her to become a nun, a year or two before she would have become a legal adult. In order to do this, she needed to go to the police station and sign a declaration stating that she released her daughter to the monastery.

"Your mother will go to the Second Coming with that paper and she will show it to Christ. What more will she need to show Him? She gave her *child* to Him," Gerontissa told the novice on her arrival at the monastery.

Like a second St. Anna, she gave up her daughter so she could live solely for the Lord; that kind of good work is hard to match.

21

KNOT TWENTY-ONE

Prayer of the Heart

FROM A YOUNG AGE, schema-nun (Yia-yia) Paraskevi wanted to become a monastic. Her parents forbade her, however, and in obedience to them she was married to a man in her village. He was not a kind man and did not treat her well. But by the grace of God she persevered "until the end" (Mark 13:13).

The couple had one daughter, and it is from her that we learned of Yia-yia's ascetical life in the world. Her daughter said that every night at exactly 10:30 PM, Yia-yia Paraskevi went out onto her small, dark balcony and said her prayers. She would do many prostrations and pray many prayer ropes. Unbeknownst to her, her young daughter would watch her through the slats in the shutters, quietly learning the art of prayer.

While living in the world, Yia-yia also did a lot of charitable works, which the nuns say greatly contributed to her state of prayer and sanctity. Once her husband died, she was finally free to follow the monastic life she had always longed to live. That is how she came to be a nun at the monastery at a much older age.

As a nun, Yia-yia Paraskevi always sat near the chanters in church. They told me that when she was first tonsured a great-schema nun, she was so fragrant that the nuns at the chanting stand almost had to cover their noses because the fragrance was so strong. This fragrance lasted for the full eight days after her tonsure. Soon afterward she started losing her memory, and it was not too long before she had advanced Alzheimer's disease.

Although Yia-yia had grown old and was no longer able to tell you who or where she was, she always maintained the spiritual character she had cultivated.

One evening a group of us were sitting together with Gerontissa and some of the sisters, with Yia-yia sitting among us for company.

"Don't think I'm crazy because my mouth won't stop moving. I can't help it, it just does that!" she told us. Occasionally she would turn her attention to us and in her whispery, low voice she would entreat us not to think badly of her mouth's movement.

"I'm sorry my mouth just won't stop saying *Kyrie Iesou Hriste eleison me!*" she told us soon after.

Many times I would see Yia-yia's mouth, with only a few teeth left, moving involuntarily. I even remember times when I would know she was walking behind me without seeing her because I could hear her distinct whisper at the word *Iesous* (Jesus).

She had prayer of the heart. She prayed night and day without needing her intellect, for her heart* prayed for her. She prayed from her heart at all times without even being aware of her surroundings. Like a second King Solomon, Yia-yia "slept" but her "heart was awake" (Song of Songs 5:2).

Despite the fact that Yia-yia could not tell you her own name, she could give you spiritual advice. Many times the sisters would go to her. "I have this or that problem," they would tell her.

"Read this topic, in this book, on that page," she informed them.

Looking up the passage Yia-yia mentioned, the sisters would be advised in exactly the manner they needed.

At other times she would give them a spiritual word to help them in their particular situation. Did she remember that she was a grown woman living in a monastery? No. Most nights she fought with the nuns to let her go home to her mother. But if anyone had a spiritual need, she knew exactly what to tell them in order to help them. This is true Orthodox spirituality; it's acquired and not forgotten.

Yia-yia was a perfect example showing us that you can lose control over your mind and memory, but that the prayer, the *ascesis*,* the good works that you have done are never erased. They seep deep into your heart and soul and remain there unto the ages of ages.

Once she had become far advanced in the disease and was hardly eating or drinking, she remained in her cell and the priest brought her Holy Communion from the Divine Liturgy.

I always found it so moving—just before the last prayers in the Divine Liturgy the priest would take the Chalice, and with a nun going before him with incense in one hand and a glass lantern with a lit candle in the other, they went to the sisters' cells.

Many times the nuns told me that after she communed, Yia-yia would ask, "Those Three, where did they go?" Or she would refuse to eat afterward—even *antidoron*.* "I don't want to eat because

I want that sweetness to stay in my heart," she would tell them.

At other times the sisters would ask Yia-yia, "How can we attain prayer of the heart?"

"Say the Jesus Prayer every day, all the time, as much as you are able. Some day years from now, it will become noetic* and enter your heart," she would answer.

The first time I heard the Greek folk song "The Prayer," I immediately thought of Yia-yia's advice. It conveys in rhyme and rhythm both the practice and the outcome of saying the Jesus Prayer. In poetic imagery it offers the essentials for acquiring prayer of the heart: a blessing, obedience, humility, and watchfulness.*

> *From Pharaoh of Egypt, slavery departing,*
> *With my guide Moses, to Sinai arriving.*
>
> *Mount Sinai to ascend! Oh how much I desire,*
> *To the holy summit's peak and the Prayer to acquire.*
>
> *May God give me patience on the harsh ascent,*
> *Fortitude, endurance, for the Prayer's acquirement.*
>
> *Primarily obedience, the Scriptures, and watchfulness*
> *Combined with holy silence enhance true prayerfulness.*
>
> *In order for you the Prayer to properly say,*
> *From your mind worldly things throw completely away.*
>
> *In the beginning be sure to say the Prayer orally,*
> *And in due time you will find you say it noetically.*
>
> *On the words of the Prayer hold full attention,*
> *For if you imagine you're in danger of delusion.*

The Prayer exasperates the one who is tempting,
Wherefore don't be disconcerted by his relentless attacking.

From the tree of prayer the sweetest fruits you receive,
Oh! What honey gushes forth you're unable to conceive.

How the Prayer works, to tell you don't ask me,
I'm unable to explain, for it's a divine mystery.

When the Prayer energizes within, continually,
Then guard it well, carefully, with much humility.

My venerable elder, my noetic Moses, guiding,
To acquire the Prayer bestow upon me your blessing.

The Prayer she gives; Christians she blesses,
The Mother of God, the Most Holy Abbess.

Mount Sinai to ascend! Oh how much I desire,
To the holy summit's peak and the Prayer to acquire.

The Holy Spirit Shall Teach You What Things to Say

SR. RAPHAELA HAD TAKEN ENGLISH language courses over fifteen years ago when she was a teenager, before coming to the monastery. Over the years she didn't have the opportunity to practice the language, so her level went down from little to non-existent.

A group of doctors from Doctors without Borders was scheduled to come to the monastery for a tour. They had called ahead and were expecting one of the nuns to give them the tour in English. Sr. Raphaela was in charge of giving tours and explaining the history of the monastery, but she had all but forgotten the small amount of English she had learned years ago. (This was before any nuns who spoke English came to the monastery, so she had no one to turn to who knew the language any better than she did.) The fact that they were all doctors added to her nervousness.

Since she was overwhelmed at the thought of conducting the tour in English, she knelt before the icon of the patron saint and prayed. She told him she needed a favor. He needed to help her.

When the day came to give the doctors the tour and explain the monastery's history, Sr. Raphaela made the sign of the cross and tried her best to explain everything in English. At the end of the tour, to her great astonishment, one of the doctors asked her, "Did you study in Europe, or perhaps in the UK? Your English is perfect!"

The other doctors agreed, and it was then she realized she had conducted the entire tour in perfect English.

She thanked the saint from the bottom of her heart. Having fulfilled her immediate need, the saint then allowed her to return to her limited knowledge of the English language. This small, but significant miracle testifies to the power of the Holy Spirit; there is no need for us to worry about what we shall say or even in what language we will need to say it!

She Cast In as Much as She Had

"I FIND IT EXTREMELY DIFFICULT to find tears when reflecting on my sins," Sr. Agathi told me one summer evening after we had finished cutting up and packaging fasting cake the sisters had made earlier that day.

"I spoke to Geronda about this. I told him I cannot get myself to the point of tears when thinking about my sins and passions. I asked him what to do about it, and he told me something that gives me comfort to this day." At this she straightened up, placed her hand on her chest and (ironically) blinked away tears.

"He told me that for a person who does not cry easily and struggles to shed tears over his or her sins, it is enough for that person to merely sigh. One deep, heartfelt sigh from a person with this kind of character can equal a lifetime of tears by someone else with a different character. This helped me so much," she said, crossing herself.

Once, while we were unpacking a box of small icons of the Wedding in Cana the sisters had ordered to make wedding favors with, Sr. Sarah told me the following story:

"There was a monk who, when he lived in the world, worked as an acrobat in a circus. At some point he decided to become a monk, but never seemed to find his niche in the monastery. He couldn't cook like some of the fathers. He couldn't chant, paint icons, or do carpentry. He felt as though he had no particular talent to offer to the Lord. The only thing he had ever been good at in his life was acrobatics.

"So one evening while praying in the church with the other fathers, he decided—in his simplicity—to offer to God the only talent he felt he had to offer. He waited for all the fathers to leave the church and hid in a shadowed corner where he was not seen by the monk who looked after the church.

"Once the ecclesiarch left the church and locked the door, the monk came out from his hiding place and went into the altar. He lifted his eyes to Christ hanging on the cross and said, 'I want to offer you my only talent.'"

Here Sr. Sarah broke off for a moment and began to cry. I had never seen her cry like this, and I assumed that she, in some way or another, saw herself in this monk.

"At this he started flipping, and jumping, and twirling. He did a whole acrobatic routine, just as he did in the circus. At the end he fell down, covered in sweat and panting. 'I'm sorry, Lord, this is all I have to offer You,' he said.

"This went on for days, weeks. Every night he hid and every night he offered to the Lord what he felt was the only talent he possessed.

"For a few nights the ecclesiarch noticed this monk was lingering behind and became curious as to why he waited to be the last one in the church. Then one night he noticed the acrobat monk didn't leave the church at all. So while the monk was hiding in his usual place, the ecclesiarch pretended to leave, but instead hid in order to see what the acrobat monk was up to.

"Thinking he was alone, the monk went into the altar and began his usual routine of flips and jumps. Seeing this the ecclesiarch was mortified and thought to himself, 'Wait till the abbot hears of this.'

"The next day the ecclesiarch told the abbot everything he had witnessed and advised the abbot to stay behind in the church to see for himself what the monk was doing in the altar. The abbot agreed do so.

"That evening the two of them hid together and watched as the monk entered the altar and did his routine. At the end, the monk lay down before the cross on the altar, as he always did, and told the Lord, 'I'm sorry, this is all I have to offer.'

"As the monk was lying on the floor panting and covered in sweat, the abbot saw the Lord Himself get down from His cross and wipe the sweat off of the monk's face, saying, 'Thank you.'

"When the abbot saw this, he became frightened and told the ecclesiarch, 'We were wrong to spy on this righteous monk. Let's get out of here.' The two of them quietly snuck out and never confronted the monk about his nightly activity."

Under normal circumstances, an abbot would of course find it reproachful for a monk to act immodestly in the altar, as this monk had done. But in this particular case the monk acted out of simplicity, pure love, and devotion, and therefore his offering was acceptable to the Lord.

In both of these stories I saw a common thread. We don't have to shed buckets of tears in order to receive mercy, nor excel in a praiseworthy handicraft in order to offer worthwhile work to the Lord. Whatever kind of prayer or work we offer can be acceptable, provided we offer *all* that we have. For, "Assuredly, I say to you that this poor widow has put in more than all those who have given to the treasury; for they all put in out of their abundance, but she out of her poverty put in all that she had, her whole livelihood" (Mark 12:43–44).

22

KNOT TWENTY-TWO

The Love of a Mother

ONE YEAR, JUST DAYS BEFORE the feast day of the patron of the monastery, I was in the kitchen helping with the dishes. I had gone into the little room in which they keep dishes to put some of the dishes away.

As I was standing in the entrance of the little room, just about to come back into the kitchen, I saw Gerontissa Philareti walk in and all the nuns surround her. I was used to seeing the nuns take her blessing, since the first time a nun or visitor sees the abbess each day they kiss her right hand. But the way they were crowding around her at that particular moment was different. They all went near her at the same time and started kissing her wherever they could reach. Some kissed her hands, others her arms, her shoulders, her head;

all of them were thanking her, and many were beginning to cry.

Gerontissa looked, for the first and only time I remember, a little embarrassed and even made a funny, playful face at one of the nuns. I was moved by this, and feeling like I was watching a very intimate, family moment, I shrank back from the doorway. I didn't want them to notice me so they would feel free to express their love and gratitude to Gerontissa. Sr. Euphemia spotted me, however, and she took me by the hand to bring me closer to Gerontissa so I could take her blessing.

"We are all thanking her," Sr. Euphemia told me, "because yesterday she left a letter and a little present on each of our pillows. In the letter she encouraged us to struggle to attain spiritual purity and told us she prayed for us to have strength for the feast day and all the work that lies ahead of us. She gave us each a cross or an icon, something special for each of us. That is why we are thanking her. We haven't seen her since she did that."

They were like small children clinging to their loving mother, and she was like a mother, bashful and humbled by the love of her children. I felt very blessed to witness such a display of love and gratitude between them.

Hidden Asceticism

IN A COENOBITIC* MONASTERY you will not likely see barefoot ascetics walking around with hair shirts. But that doesn't mean strict asceticism* isn't practiced there. When you live with a lot of people, and you have a constant stream of visitors, you have to be creative about your asceticism. Here are the basic ascetical practices that I witnessed at the monastery.

The nuns work from around eight-thirty in the morning until around ten or eleven at night, frequently later. Their jobs are not easy, and most young men who come to help are not able to keep up with them.

I remember one nun's brother once visited her, and afterward he came to stay with us in Thessaloniki for a few days. He was twenty-nine years old, and when he arrived at our apartment he was exhausted.

"I don't know how they do it! I am an athlete. I have trained and done triathlons, and I have never been so completely exhausted as I was from the work at the monastery! Gerontissa must just pray for them on her prayer rope, and God must give them superhuman strength in order to do all the work they do," he told us.

This is very true. It was only when people came to help the sisterhood, especially with hard manual labor, and were not able to keep up, that the nuns realized the strength they have comes from God. The saint of the monastery is always there encouraging and helping them to restore and maintain his house.

For breakfast, since they do not eat together, each eats according to what she needs. For example, one time I happened to be eating my breakfast in their dining hall while a few of them were eating. One of them who sat with me ate a piece of bread with oil and lemon on it, and had cocoa for a drink. For lunch they always eat a proper meal together with vegetables, fish, dairy products (when allowed), and bread. For dinner, once again, those who need to eat, eat according to their particular need.

Every evening in church they pray the Vespers service, Compline, the Akathist hymn to the Mother of God, and a Supplication service to a saint.

After their work is done, they take shifts throughout the night attending to the older nuns who are no longer able to take care of themselves.

They do Matins on their prayer rope, which consists of about 1,500 Jesus Prayers. They also pray whichever Hours are not read in the church on their prayer ropes. Then they have their personal prayer rule, which consists of prostrations, Jesus Prayers while making crosses on each knot of their prayer rope, other prayers on the prayer rope, and possibly readings from spiritual books and other written prayers, such as a Supplicatory Canon or an Akathist Hymn.

Each has her own personalized prayer rule, and no one inquires or knows that of the others. They perform this rule at some point in the night, either before sleeping, after sleeping, or in between hours of sleeping. Each chooses to pray at the time she feels is best.

The general rule is for the nuns to sleep only four hours a night. Of course, there are always exceptions based on health and other factors. The abbess regulates these things according to necessity. I remember one of the nuns telling me how she always loved reading stories about Russian monastics because they are so ascetical. She wanted to model her own life after theirs, but due to her health she was not able to accomplish even the basic ascetical practices at her own monastery. She told me that although the rule is to sleep only four hours a night, the sisterhood's spiritual father told her she should sleep six hours. It grieved her that it was still difficult for her to function on a full six hours.

Other sisters try to take on ascetic feats that are concealed. For this reason I don't know a lot of what they do personally, but I do know some of them don't wash their hair. I would find that very difficult. I learned this from one of the sisters, who told me that when Gerontissa was a young nun, she didn't wash her hair for twelve years. Her hair never smelled bad, and her scalp never itched.

"For asceticism some nuns don't wash their hair. But it can make your scalp extremely itchy!" the sister informed me, and by saying that she gave herself away, because many times I noticed her intensely scratching her head.

The only other hidden asceticism I knew of was done by one of the sisters whom the Lord decided to take to Himself when she was still a young woman. Her name was Evpraxia. Her cell mate, Sr. Monica, told me she used to wake up in the night or after siesta and see Sr. Evpraxia sleeping on the floor.

"I used to tell her, 'Evpraxia! Get up! Sleep on your bed! What are you doing on the floor?' because I was only a teenager then," Sr. Monica told me.

"It helps my back," Sr. Evpraxia always responded.

To me, the nuns' most ascetical feat was the layers of clothing they wore. Besides their regular underwear, they wear undershirts and undershorts, and their pajamas (a blouse and skirt) on top of that. Over their pajamas they wear their everyday long-sleeved shirt, skirt, and vest.

Underneath their regular headscarves, tonsured nuns wear little hats, in keeping with the rule of St. Pachomias's monastic habit. When they are in church, they wear another garment that looks like a long cloak on top of their regular rasso, and another long headscarf. They wear all of this all year round, even when it's over a hundred degrees in the summer!

But the point of telling you all this isn't for me to know all the ways in which they practice asceticism and deny themselves for the glory of God. That is for God to know. I wanted to share the basic ascetical acts they do to illustrate that monasticism really is death to oneself.

Monastics give up all freedoms to live for Christ. For their entire life they make sacrifices in order to obey Christ and struggle to keep His commandments. I may sacrifice my time to help someone with something, but afterwards I return to my schedule and my comforts.

They do not have the option of returning to their personal comforts. They left those behind when they left the world.

They entered the monastery and it was as though they entered their tomb. This is the monastic mindset. They are still joyful, laugh, love, and smile, but they no longer live for themselves in any way. They cannot wear what they want, read the books they want, take the day off when they want, eat when or what they want. Yet monasticism offers freedom.

Like everyone, monastics fall at times and struggle with the same sins and passions we in the world do. But they do it in a community that is able to tell you when you are straying, a community that has a spiritual mother to inform you which thoughts are garbage, which ones are from God, and how to proceed to make it across the finish line without getting tripped up by the wiles of the devil.

Instead of family, they have saints; instead of husbands, Christ; instead of friends, each other; instead of children, virtues; instead of paychecks, prayer ropes; instead of outward beauty, internal purity; instead of perfume, myrrh; instead of wealth, holy icons and relics. They are as St. Paul describes: "poor, yet making many rich; as having nothing, and *yet* possessing all things" (2 Cor. 6:10).

I have read many articles and heard many homilies that praise family life and downplay monasticism. Yes, you *can* become a saint in the home. But why regard family life and monasticism as opposed to each other? Instead of seeing life in the world as somehow utterly disconnected from life in the monastery, why don't we take what we learn from monastics and reasonably apply it to our own lives?

I have heard one too many times that St. Anthony the Great was relevant to the world, stressing how he came out of the desert and into the world twice in his life. He was an ascetic. He had nothing to do with the world. Why do we have to drag him into the world? Leave him in the desert where he chose to live. His relationship to the world was one based on prayer, his only and most vital connection to life in the world. Why not, instead, bring a grain of sand from the desert into our home? Why not practice asceticism, hidden and in the home? Just as the nuns conceal their asceticism, so can we.

There is no need to go easy on ourselves because we live in the world. The world goes easy enough on us as it is. To take hold of what we find helpful in the monastery and tweak it to apply to our own life offers us many spiritual benefits. Let's leave the monastics on their pillars and not try to pull them down. Let's instead build our own small pillar in the middle of the city. Let's take from their example and do just as they do.

"If you want to be perfect," the Lord said, "go, sell what you have and give to the poor, and you will have treasure in heaven; and come, follow Me" (Matt. 19:21). Monastics have sold all they had in hopes of becoming perfect. That doesn't mean we in the world cannot join them in perfection by denying our own selves, keeping the commandments, and cutting off our will. If the nuns taught me anything, they taught me that cutting off one's will is the hardest but best form of asceticism. This ascetic feat is at all times readily available to us in the world: at work, at home, in our parish. Christ's saying doesn't mean we cannot be saved if we don't become ascetics in the world, but it does mean we won't become perfect.

Work in Me a Sign unto Good

ONE EVENING SOME FRIENDS of ours came to the monastery to attend the Vespers service. At that time their baby girl was just getting used to wobbling around as toddlers do. She walked back and forth from where her mother was standing to the chanter's stand. This went on during the whole service.

As Vespers was finishing, the baby once again walked toward the chanter's stand just as the nuns were stepping down. The baby found herself encircled by the nuns and, I suppose out of fun, one of the sisters bowed to the baby. Instantly the whole group of nuns followed her lead and all bowed, touching the floor.

When an abbess is in the center of the church, usually at the end of a service or just before receiving Holy Communion, she stands and turns toward the sisterhood. As she begins to bow toward them, they all bow and touch the ground before her.

"Maybe she'll become a great abbess," Sr. Constantina told the parents, smiling broadly.

The sisters' gesture toward the baby girl may have merely been a playful one, but it could also signify something more. I suppose only time will tell.

KNOT TWENTY-THREE

Story Time with Sr. Evlogia

O NE EVENING IN LATE SPRING, a group of us who were staying at the monastery sat with Sr. Evlogia, one of the older nuns, in the reception area. We all spread out in a semicircle on the padded benches and chairs while she sat in the middle, facing us. This was a rare but memorable experience. She told us many different stories that night for our spiritual benefit, and I will share a few of them here.

She first told us about a family she knew from Germany. The woman was Greek and the man was German; she was an Orthodox Christian and he was Catholic. Their daughter had become very ill, and the mother decided to take her to the island of Aegina to the monastery where St. Nektarios lived the final years of his life, and where he was buried. The husband accompanied his wife and child to supplicate the saint to heal their daughter. Through the saint's prayers, the young girl was cured.

On returning to Germany, the father saw St. Nektarios in a dream. "I want you to become an Orthodox priest!" the saint instructed him.

The man was perplexed. He did not doubt that it was indeed St. Nektarios and that he truly did want him to become a priest; he merely did not know how to go about fulfilling the saint's request. He was not even an Orthodox Christian, let alone in a position to become an Orthodox priest.

So he called the local Orthodox bishop in order to first become a catechumen.* After some time he was baptized, and when his studies were complete, he became a priest. On the day of the man's ordination, he was granted to see St. Nektarios in the sanctuary with him. What's more amazing still is from that day on, the German priest never once served Divine Liturgy without St. Nektarios visibly accompanying him in the sanctuary.

WHEN SR. EVLOGIA WAS A CHILD, she became ill, and her mother and father took her to the island of Tinos. They went to the same church where Sr. Silouani and her husband had gone to pray that God give them a child. The church housed the famous miracle-working icon of the Theotokos called the Great Joy. Each year on the Feast of the Dormition of the Mother of God, crowds of thousands come to this church. Sr. Evlogia and her parents, as well as many other families, remained in the church after the Vespers service until the following morning.

While they were in the church that night, suddenly above the iconostasis stood a woman in the air, dressed as a nun and blessing the crowds with her two hands the way a bishop does. However, only the children could see her.

KNOT TWENTY-THREE

"Panagia! It's Panagia!" all the children began to shout at once. The Lady Theotokos came down from the air and started walking through the crowds. The children kept calling out, "Panagia! Panagia!"

"Where? Where is Panagia?" the adults asked.

"There she is! Over there!" the children would call out.

She walked through the crowds blessing everyone, and then she disappeared. Sr. Evlogia said she even remembers the church officials coming and writing down the faithful's accounts of the miracle.

"What did she look like?" I asked, wide-eyed and excited.

Sr. Evlogia shrugged. "Like a nun," she said. "She had on a headscarf like we wear and long robes. She looked like a nun."

SR. EVLOGIA PROCEEDED TO TELL us some dreams that two faithful villagers experienced. The first dream took place sometime after the monastery was left to the care of only one nun. The villager who saw the dream was particularly grieved that the village's beloved monastery was no longer flourishing, and she often prayed for God to revitalize the community there.

While asleep she saw the patron saint of the monastery. He was standing in the middle of a group of women. These women were all wearing white robes with red crosses on the front and back. Their hair was down and loose and very long. They were holding hands and going around the patron saint together as though they were dancing.

The woman understood this to mean that the monastery would once again become a place full of monastics and, more specifically, great-schema nuns. For when a nun is tonsured into the great schema, she wears a baptismal robe with a red cross. Being tonsured into the great schema is a second baptism in which the monastic's sins are once again completely washed away.

For the service, the nun lets down her hair (which is usually kept pinned up in a series of braids in the form of crosses). In the dream, the nuns' hair was very long because nuns do not cut their hair from the time they enter the monastery. The woman from the village glorified God for having received that dream, for she understood that more nuns would come to re-establish the monastic life in the monastery.

The second dream was experienced by another villager. In her dream she was walking up towards the monastery's gate. Before it she saw a bishop holding a bishop's staff—a symbol of the shepherd's crosier—with countless sheep around him. Beside him she saw what she thought was a nun. Only this nun wore her headscarf so low it covered her eyes. Approaching them, she heard the bishop say to the nun, "Put these few sheep inside my monastery, for they are the only ones that do my will."

As the woman got closer to the bishop and the nun, she realized it was not a bishop but Jesus Christ the Lord, and that the woman was the Mother of our Lord. Realizing this, she said, "Panagia, why do you cover your eyes?"

"I cover my eyes because I am ashamed to look at the world because of the sins of the people," the Mother of God responded, gesturing toward the village.

It may seem strange, but of all the stories Sr. Evlogia told us, this last story had the strongest effect on me. Once we wished each other good night, I returned to the guestroom with the two other young women who were staying with me, and that phrase continued to echo in my mind: "I am ashamed to look at the world because of the sins of the people."

I realize that sometimes we can just be oversensitive, but at other times I really do believe God speaks to us in ways that will help to rouse us from our spiritual slumber. I was so affected by that phrase that immediately after Sr. Evlogia said it, my face burned and was most certainly bright red. Of course the dream was not mine and the Mother of God was not speaking merely of my own personal sins, but that is how I felt.

My friend Alexia noticed that I seemed a bit quiet and asked me what I was thinking.

"I feel as though Panagia was ashamed to look at the world because of *my* sins," I told her.

"Constantina, it wasn't because—" I could hear in her voice that she was downplaying what I felt, and I cut her off.

"No, the truth is if she is ashamed to look at the world because of our sin, it is as much my fault as it is anyone else's."

"You're right, I'm sorry," she said, understanding if not from my words, then from my quivering voice, that I felt strongly about it.

An Act of Mercy

MRS. MARIA, SR. SILOUANI'S SISTER, was once telling Gerontissa about a friend she had who was wheelchair bound but wanted very much to visit a monastery and receive the blessing of the abbess. With great care her husband took her to a monastery, but due to some unknown reason the abbess could not make herself available to speak with the woman. Mrs. Maria was complaining about this, and Gerontissa told her, "Why don't you bring her here, then?"

"But Gerontissa, the cobblestone courtyard—she wouldn't be able to get across it in her wheelchair!"

"That doesn't matter," Gerontissa told her. "The sisters will carry her in her wheelchair, and we can sit and chat."

Mrs. Maria was obviously enthused by what Gerontissa said because she feared her friend would not live much longer and wanted to help grant her request.

The nuns were used to carrying wheelchairs with people in them. Ever since Sr. Markella became wheelchair bound, every day for years they carried her from her cell to the building with the kitchen and dining hall so she could do a little work, whatever she was able to do, and share the common meal with the sisterhood. And every evening they carried her back to her cell.

In Christ Jesus I Begot You

IT WAS A BRIGHT, WARM SUNDAY MORNING in early September when I had the blessing of seeing Archimandrite Evsevios one last time. He had traveled with two of his spiritual children to visit the monastery. Being a hieromonk, he attended the Divine Liturgy in the sanctuary behind the iconostasis. However, Constantine, his spiritual child, filled with loving concern, was not far away. He stood just in front of the embroidered curtain of the right deacon's door, in case the elder needed him.

Elder Evsevios was dying. He had already written a letter to each of his spiritual children to inform them he would no longer be able to fulfill his duty as a spiritual father and that he was releasing all of them to find another spiritual father.

Understandably, this filled his spiritual children with much sadness and grief. Their father was leaving them. They were being orphaned. Of course, God provides for us in all situations, and only He decides when it is best for our spiritual fathers to leave this world, this "veil of tears." But Elder Evsevios's spiritual children loved him very much, and out of devotion they did not want to replace him before his death. Obedience, however, overrode their personal desires, and they accepted the elder's decision. This did not mean, though, that they wouldn't be there until the end.

Word spread quickly that the elder was leaving his hermitage in order to attend the Divine Liturgy at the monastery. The nave of the church quickly filled with his spiritual children. After the Liturgy ended they all stood, waiting. Constantine brought the elder out of the sanctuary and into the nave, and everyone crowded round. They left space for him to walk through as those closest to him bent low to take his blessing.

Many women were wiping tears away, and even I, who had only met the elder one other time, found it difficult not to cry on their behalf. I thought of how I would feel if my spiritual father had released me and told me to find another. I have met many wonderful and holy people, pious priests, and amazing theology professors. But no one is quite like one's own spiritual father.

We followed the elder out into the courtyard. We walked toward the guesthouse, where the sisters had put out a chair for the elder to sit on. He sat, and like little sparrows hungry for food, his spiritual children all formed a circle around him. "For though you might have ten thousand instructors in Christ, yet *you do* not *have* many fathers; for in Christ Jesus I have begotten you through the gospel" (1 Cor. 4:15).

I stayed with them long enough to take the elder's blessing and see him smile at all of us. I desperately wanted to hear what he was saying, but his voice had grown weak with age, and the laughter of the children playing near the fountain made it difficult for me to hear him.

I stepped back, took one last look at that living saint, and held his spiritual children in my heart. If he were my spiritual father, I'd have crowded around too and never taken my eyes off him, especially if he told me he was leaving to take the last journey home.

In November of the same year, Elder Evsevios fell asleep in the Lord, but doubtless he remains forever in the thoughts and hearts of all his devoted spiritual children. And, of course, I fully believe he keeps company with the saints and angels. May his memory be eternal!

Precious in the Sight of the Lord is the Death of His Saints

IT WAS THE LAST WEEK in August, and it was clear to the whole sisterhood that Yia-yia Paraskevi was coming to the end of the race. She was refusing nearly all food and drink, so the sisters called her daughter and grandchildren to come and bid her farewell.

Just before Yia-yia fell asleep in the Lord, she became a different person. Or rather, I should say, she came back to herself. Suddenly she was much more cognizant than she had been in recent years; she remembered who everyone was and what their names were. Although she rested a lot in those last days, she also was awake long enough for the sisterhood to take notice of this change.

"I'm leaving," she said on Sunday afternoon, three days before she departed.

During those last three days, Sr. Irene, who was her primary attendant, saw that she kept reaching toward the icon of her patron saint above her bed.

One time she cupped her hand as though something was being placed in it. Drawing her hand back, she wiped her face as though she had some kind of cloth or ointment to apply.

Another time she reached her hand toward her saint's icon and pulled it back as though she were holding something spherical. She brought her hand to her mouth and started making the motions of biting and chewing. After "eating" for some time, she finally finished by licking her fingers as though there were some kind of juice left on them.

Who knows what things Yia-yia saw or heard in those last days, those last moments. Such things are mysteries to us, the uninitiated. But "holy things are for the holy," and Yia-yia, being holy, received holy things.

The day Yia-yia fell asleep, Gerontissa came to see her in the morning. For the first time in a long time, she grabbed Gerontissa's hand to take her blessing. It had been years since she recognized Gerontissa as her abbess. The nuns all felt it was a sign that she was taking a blessing so she could leave. And she knew the sisters as well; she recognized them and knew their names.

That afternoon, the first of September, the first day of the new ecclesiastical year, her breathing became thick. Hearing the death rattle, Gerontissa had Sr. Irene call all the nuns to come and say goodbye. They all came at once. Bowing low, each asked her forgiveness and took her blessing.

Then Yia-yia pursed her lips, as though something were being offered her to drink, and made a face displaying displeasure, as though the drink were bitter. She laid her head on her pillow and slightly opened her mouth. Then her soul departed.

"It was the cup of death," Sr. Euphemia told me afterward. "The Archangel Michael comes to everyone at their death and gives them a bitter drink in order to make the soul depart."

The sisters immediately set to work, preparing Yiayia's body so that all the friends of the monastery and relatives of the nuns could come and bid her farewell. No one slept that night. They were too busy with all the preparations and prayers to bother with sleep.

"The strange thing was, no one was tired. No one felt like she had been up all night. We all felt joy and peace. It was a blessing from Yia-yia," Sr. Sarah told me.

They washed her body with a mixture of water and wine, and clothed her in a white gown with her full monastic robe and schema on top. They placed the candle she was given at her great-schema tonsure in her hands along with her long prayer rope. Then they laid her on the funeral bier.

They placed her in the center of the church, her body facing the altar. They placed a small table near her head. On it an oil lamp was lit which was not extinguished until after her burial.

Her whole body was covered by a large, embroidered cloth that bore the great schema. Only her face was visible, her head being covered in her monastic headscarf. They rested an icon of Christ's Harrowing of Hell on her chest. At no point was Yia-yia's body left in the church unattended. They each took turns throughout the night reading the Psalter next to her.

I am told the funeral was very beautiful. In fact, the sisters told me a friend of the monastery had commented afterward, "If only people knew how beautiful the funeral service for a great-schema nun is, they would desire the great schema, just for the service alone."

However, to my great sorrow, I was not in Greece when Yia-yia fell asleep in the Lord, and so I missed the opportunity to bid her farewell. I hope that someday, through the sisters' prayers, I may be granted a reunion not only with Yia-yia Paraskevi but with all the righteous who have gone before me. Together with the saints, may she intercede for us!

24

KNOT TWENTY-FOUR

A Black Animal that Walks in the Air

ONE NIGHT WE WERE ALL in the church for a vigil. I was sitting on one of the stasidia in an area that was particularly dark. The only source of light in the whole church was the candles and oil lamps in the nave and the candle box in the narthex. It was early summer, so the sisters had left the door open for some fresh air to enter. Unfortunately, something else entered with it.

While I was sitting down, I felt something fly towards my face and then up into the air. I jerked but thankfully didn't scream like a lunatic (a trait I regretfully inherited from my mother). It flew around a bit more, and I took the woolen shawl I was wearing and pulled it up over my head as an attempt at protection. Suddenly the thing became visible, and from the light of the oil lamps I saw the disturbing form of bat's wings. They were almost transparent. I could see the light through them a little.

Of course, the nun sitting two stasidia over hardly budged while I was trying to prevent myself from running out screaming and flailing. I quickly got up and went to tell Sr. Silouani, who sat by the door since she was in charge of the candles. However, I could neither remember the word for "bat" nor the verb for "fly," so I frantically said to her, "There is an animal—a black animal—that walks in the air! It doesn't walk actually, but I can't remember the verb for what it does. It's in the church—a black animal that walks in the air!"

Concerned and not understanding me, Sr. Silouani got up to come into the nave to see what I was talking about. Just then Sr. Theologia came over and said to me: "A bat? Did you see a bat?"

"Yes!" I said, remembering the word when I heard it, and relieved someone understood.

When Sr. Silouani heard the word *bat* she busted up. She struggled very hard to contain her laughter. Holding my arm, she bent over with her hand on her mouth. "Constandia, a bat? A bat?"

"Yes," I said with a frown.

She turned a lamp on in the narthex so that no more bats would come in. I returned to my seat, hoping the light would protect me. Sr. Silouani returned to hers and, I hope, managed to regain some form of concentration.

Why Not Receiving a Blessing Can Be a Blessing

MRS. OLGA, THE MOTHER OF the twins, is from Switzerland. She married a Greek man and years later decided to accept the Orthodox faith. At some point she decided she wanted to be baptized. She asked her close friend if she would be willing to become her godmother. This friend was a spiritual daughter of the monastery's spiritual father, so she called him and asked for his blessing. He told her, "No, Olga should go to the monastery where my spiritual children are nuns and ask the abbess there to become her godmother."

The friend shared this with Mrs. Olga and so she, her husband, and their young girls visited the monastery. They told Gerontissa Philareti what the spiritual father had said, and she agreed to become Mrs. Olga's godmother.

This is how the family began visiting the monastery and becoming close to Gerontissa and the sisterhood. At that time the twins were being tutored by two cousins. They mentioned to their tutors that they visited this monastery, and that is how Sr. Akakia and Sr. Agathi also came to know about the monastery. When the twins were seventeen years old, they became novices with their parents' permission, just after Sr. Akakia and Sr. Agathi did. And so, merely by the woman's act of obedience to her spiritual father, four young women learned about the monastery and later became nuns there.

He Shall Crush the Serpent's Skull

THERE ARE MANY SNAKES IN Greece. Thankfully they are mostly outside of the city. But unfortunately, they are in plenty in and around the monastery. The sisterhood is careful to put out snake poison, but it has never cut down on the number of snakes that manage to get into the monastery. The sisters can't just allow poisonous snakes to be in the monastery, since there are many visitors and loads of young children often visiting. If someone gets bitten, the nearest hospital is a long way away.

I had been at the monastery a few times when people came screaming, "*Fidi! Fidi!*," warning the sisters there was a snake in the courtyard.

This always resulted in at least three nuns grabbing shovels and heading in the direction of the serpent in order to kill it.

I remember the sisters telling us about snakes that coil back and pounce on top of you, blind snakes with thick skin, baby snakes that have no control over how much venom they put into their victims, and long snakes that whip you with their tail as though it's a leather switch.

"If you see one, just make the sign of the cross over it," they would say nonchalantly, revealing their unwavering faith.

"Could you at least tell us what the most poisonous ones look like?" I'd ask them.

"Some are brown, some are grayish . . . They're a variety of colors," they would answer.

ONE AFTERNOON, A FRIEND of Sr. Epomoni was with her outside the monastery walls, near the garden. Sr. Epomoni was going to head back to the monastery while her friend was going to head down the path to the garden. They both started walking in opposite directions when Sr. Epomoni turned back to say something to her friend. She saw a long snake lying coiled up before her friend on the path. She didn't say anything to her friend just then because she was so close to the serpent, she knew any distraction might cause her to step right onto it. Instead, Sr. Epomoni quickly made the sign of the cross over the snake from where she was standing, and her friend unknowingly stepped right over it. When the friend was a safe distance away, Sr. Epomoni called out to her, "Look behind you at what was in your path. You stepped right over it!" Of course on seeing the large snake the woman was in disbelief.

A FEW DAYS AFTER THAT event, late one evening when we were sitting together in the courtyard under the stars, Gerontissa treated us to ice cream. I loved the times she had Sr. Lydia go into the freezer and bring out a box of various ice creams, a gift from Sr. Silouani's friend. (Donating things like dish soap, hand soap, detergent, and coffee to monasteries is very helpful, especially because they use these things a lot for their guests. Giving things like ice cream and little chocolates is just plain fun.)

We were just finishing up our ice cream when one of the sisters came running into the courtyard. She announced that Sr. Irene had found a large snake in the garage and needed some nuns to help her kill it. I certainly wasn't going to miss a chance to see a snake like that, being from Atlantic Canada where we only have things like small garter snakes. So my sister-in-law Catherine and I took off with the nuns for the garage outside the monastery.

When we arrived, we saw Sr. Irene searching the garage with a small flashlight.

"I lost it, sisters, I'm sorry. I lost it," she told us.

Having just driven back to the monastery from the village, Sr. Irene was opening the door to the garage in order to put the car inside when she spotted the snake at the foot of the door. She always checked for snakes right away because they often stayed close to the door. There were no lights in the garage, so she used the flashlight on her keychain. Instead of keeping her flashlight on the snake and waiting for the other nuns to arrive to help her, she took a nearby shovel and tried to pin the snake herself. However, just as she went to strike the snake, her flashlight flew out of her hand, and her blow missed the serpent. Thankfully it did not strike her, but it did get away. For days she was upset with herself for presuming to pin the snake on her own and not waiting for the sisters' help.

We had brought large flashlights and shovels with us, but when I saw the rugs rolled up at the back of the garage, I thought for certain we would never find it. There were about seven of us, and everyone started searching for the snake. I was hesitant to go too far inside the garage and kept my skirt wrapped around my legs as though that would somehow protect me. After about five minutes of searching, Sr. Irene spotted it. She took the shovel and with all her might pinned the snake down. Sr. Seraphima and Sr. Monica rushed to kill it by striking it with their shovels.

"Constantina! Bring the light closer!" Sr. Seraphima shouted.

I drew in with the large flashlight. The snake was in an awkward position, in a corner just beside a cabinet. It was a particular kind that is blind but has tough, thick skin. That is why they couldn't sever it easily. It was like trying to cut a slack rubber band by striking it with a shovel.

Sr. Marina came running from the other side of the garage. Eager to help, she grabbed the flashlight out of my hands and went in closer. She put the flashlight down, grabbed a shovel from against the wall, and lit into the snake. I was taken aback by her courage. She rushed straight into battle with the resilient serpent. It took them nearly two full minutes to kill it. Afterward they held up the snake for Catherine and me to examine. Its various wounds were visible. They had won the war!

The whole event made a huge impact on me. I felt as though I were watching the nuns' spiritual life played out live in front of me. They were brave, fierce, and strong, just as soldiers should be. That night I immediately wrote down my impressions of the event and resolved never to allow the image of Sr. Marina charging into battle to fade from my memory. I wanted the courage to fight as she did, to fearlessly face the "serpent" and slay it.

KNOT TWENTY-FIVE

Made in Germany

A SMALL GROUP OF PEOPLE from Germany stopped by one day to see the monastery and take a look at the museum since they had been hiking on the nearby trails in the mountain earlier that day. When Sr. Silouani and her husband were younger, they both worked in Germany, so she knew some German.

Sr. Silouani, who was very charming and got along with everyone, greeted the women in their native tongue when they entered the bookstore. One of them struck up a conversation with her, and the next thing I knew, Sr. Silouani was coming over to the cash register to get a pen and paper and explaining their conversation to me.

"She's going to send us a pair of shoes from Germany," she told me. One of the sisters had some problems with her back, and the best shoes for her were Birkenstocks. Since they aren't available in Greece, Sr. Silouani asked the woman if she would be willing to send a pair from Germany.

"Of course," the woman told her. "I'd be happy to."

"Great," Sr. Silouani exclaimed. "I'll write down our address and the size of shoe the sister needs. We'll go over to the office together and I'll give you some money for the shoes," she told the German woman.

"And what is *your* size?" she asked Sr. Silouani.

"Oh, no, I don't need a pair, just the one sister does," Sr. Silouani answered.

"I know, but I'd like to get you a pair too," she insisted. "And I will not accept a cent from you. I want to send you and the other sister a pair out of my own pocket," she explained to Sr. Silouani's surprise.

At the persistence of the woman Sr. Silouani gave in and told her her own size as well.

Meanwhile, I watched all of this with amusement. Sr. Silouani had such a way about her. She brought out the good in so many people. Many times I had witnessed people do amazing charitable acts after speaking with Sr. Silouani. Her own open and loving character caused people to reflect her kindness.

About six months later, I asked Sr. Silouani, "Whatever happened to those Birkenstocks from Germany?" She started laughing, finding it amusing that I remembered the incident.

"She sent them!"

"She *did?*" I asked, surprised.

"Yeah, she really did! I didn't know if she would, but she did! So we sent her a Christmas card, and we'll send her one at Pascha too," she said, smiling and patting my back.

"Perhaps she'll receive Orthodoxy in return for her charity," I said.

KNOT TWENTY-FIVE

Inherent Spirituality in an Orthodox Country

AFTER LUNCH ONE AFTERNOON, Georgia, who was also staying at the monastery for the weekend, was speaking with Elder Isidoros in our guest room. I sat on my bed and read while they spoke. Finishing up their conversation, Elder Isidoros gave her some oil on a cotton ball and told her the same thing he had said to me the day before: "Say the Jesus Prayer as much as you can, and if you want, don't watch television!"

She told him her family hadn't had a television in the house for years and he, in his characteristic humorous way, said, "You don't?! Well, just wait a second! Let's see what else I can give you!" She looked at me and we both laughed. He started feeling around in his bag.

"Here, take a prayer rope!" he exclaimed, passing her a thirty-three-knot prayer rope with a small red bead.

"And what about me, Geronda? I don't have a television either," I said, teasing.

"Here, you can have one too, and here's one for your husband, and—hold on—" he continued groping around in his black bag. "Give this to Fr. Luke, your spiritual father."

"May it be blessed, Geronda," I said, hastily getting up and kissing his hand as he passed me the prayer ropes.

"Well, I think I'm going to go to my cell to lie down. Constantina, will you take me?"

"Of course, Geronda!" I said, more than willing to have the blessing of assisting the blind elder to get around.

As we were exiting the room and walking into the main gallery, I saw a young couple. Figuring from their expressions they didn't know who Elder Isidoros was, I said, "Would you like to take the papouli's blessing?"

They both stood up, took his hand and kissed it. Elder Isidoros, not understanding that they were just a couple who came to visit the monastery, thought (since so many come to see him) that they wanted to meet with him and asked, "Do you want to speak with me?"

"We've come to see Gerontissa and Sr. Paisia," the young woman answered.

"I'm sorry, I'm sorry. Good, good, see Gerontissa," the elder said immediately, stepping back and gesturing apologetically.

He squeezed my hand as we were turning to go, and I could tell he was embarrassed. How was he to know they hadn't come for him, the poor papouli! We continued in the direction of his cell. I opened the door for him and helped him to his bed. I took his blessing and shut the door. When I came back into the gallery on the way to my room, I saw that the young woman was crying.

"Who was that Geronda?" they both asked me.

"He's a monk from Philotheou Monastery on Mount Athos. He's very holy. He works miracles," I told them, pulling out a chair to sit down.

"That was a very significant thing that happened just now when he asked if we wanted to speak with him. We should have said yes! I didn't realize," the young woman said, wiping tears from her cheeks while the young man stroked her shoulder.

You see just how sensitive Greeks can be? This couple wasn't particularly "spiritual"; I found out later they were just learning about the Church, and the young man didn't even know what Philotheou was. Yet they both had the natural spiritual sensitivity that I often saw in Greeks. It's as if the sheer grace of their baptism preserves grace within them, deep down in their hearts. And the fact that, whether they know it or not, they live on sanctified ground—ground that has been purified by the blood of countless martyrs and the tears of countless ascetics, their very ancestors—also helps a lot.

"I can ask him if he will see you if you'd like," I told them.

"Yes, please ask him," the woman said quickly.

I walked back to the cell the elder was staying in and knocked on the door.

"Through the prayers of the Holy Fathers," I said (the proper thing to say when entering an occupied room or cell in a monastery). "Geronda, the young lady we just met, she's crying."

"Yeah so. How am I to blame?" he responded, with his distinct humor.

"No, Geronda," I said smiling. "I think it was grace, I think it was from the Holy Spirit, they want to speak with you."

"They said they wanted to speak with Gerontissa, so they should speak with Gerontissa," he answered.

He said this out of humility, because to him it would be interfering and overreaching to speak with them since they came to speak with the abbess. But due to my *unique* Canadian sensitivity, I was uncomfortable at the prospect of telling someone something that would potentially upset them. So, out of nervousness I started saying in English: "Okay, okay, okay."

"No, not okay, *endaxi!*" the elder yelled. He had been correcting my Greek all week, and he had already told me the day before, "You will not say *okay*, you will say *endaxi!*" (the Greek word for okay).

"Yes, of course. Endaxi," I corrected myself.

"No, give me your little hand!" he said.

I gave him my hand and he playfully slapped it.

Still nervous and not wanting to have to tell the couple that the elder said he would not speak with them, I tried asking again. "So, just to be clear, you won't speak with them?"

"If they ask Gerontissa and she says it's blessed, I will speak with them, but they need to ask her first," he answered.

Relieved by this, I unwittingly responded, "Okay."

"No! Not okay!" he once again playfully scolded.

"Give me your hair! Where is your hair?" I knelt down and put my hair in the blind elder's hands. He pulled it.

"There! Now, say *endaxi!*"

"Endaxi! Endaxi!" I said quickly, laughing and getting up off the ground.

I told the couple what the elder told me. Later that day I saw them speaking to him, so it all worked out.

This story still makes me smile, as does the simplicity, humility, and extreme humor of Elder Isidoros, the blind monk from Mount Athos.

If Your Eye Causes You to Sin, Pluck It Out

"I WAS STRUGGLING WITH SOME proud thoughts. I don't even remember with what exactly. I thought I chanted the Psalter well, and some other things. But really I can't remember them," Sr. Euphemia began. We had been speaking about various humiliating situations that help rid us of bad thoughts and unwanted behaviors.

"I confided in Gerontissa a few times about these proud thoughts. After confessing them a third time, she told me I needed to make a prostration to every nun after lunch and confess my thoughts to each one.

"During lunch I was so nervous I couldn't eat. What was I going to do? I had no appetite, but I made myself eat.

"The time came for me to complete my penance, and so I walked to the door and got down on the floor. Gerontissa was the first to pass. Before I could confess my thoughts aloud, she said, 'What are you doing down there? I didn't tell you to get down there. Get up on the table and make your prostrations.'

"So I walked over to the table we have in the trapeza with nothing on it and I climbed up. I made a prostration and started confessing my thoughts: 'Sisters, I have proud thoughts. I think I chant the Psalter well,' I said, and whatever other things I was thinking at that time.

"Some of the more sensitive sisters tried to comfort me. I was up on the table crying and they were saying, 'It's okay, Sister, I have had those thoughts too. Don't worry, Gerontissa is doing this for your own good!'

"Through tears I said, 'I know, I'm okay'," she said, laughing. "But, really, it helped a lot! Actions like that burn the devil because he can't stand humility. And afterward the thoughts left me. Really, I can't even remember them anymore! Penances like that get rid of all those problems," she said, smiling broadly.

Hurry Hard!

ONE SUMMER AFTERNOON THE NUNS had taken out all the rugs in the monastery to wash them. We laid them outside of the monastery on the slanted road. Three of us put on rain boots, grabbed some buckets, soap, and brooms, and headed out.

We filled the buckets with soapy water and had the scrubbing brooms at the ready. The plan was that one nun would slowly pour the soapy water down the rug and I, on one side of the rug, and a nun on the opposite side, would scrub.

Once the sister emptied the bucket, we quickly followed the soapy water down to the bottom of the rug, brushing the suds firmly into the carpet. It was great fun! It reminded me a lot of curling, a sport that is popular in Canada. I wanted so badly to explain this to the nuns, but they had a difficult time understanding the concept of a sport played on ice with two brooms and a rock.

"You mean you walk on the ice—with shoes on?"

"Yes," I said. "And there's a rock, with a handle, that someone slides down the ice."

"A rock? You slide a rock down the ice?" they asked, bewildered.

"Yes. And then the one sliding the rock shouts, 'Hurry hard!' and the two other team members, the ones with brooms, go before the rock and brush the ice so that the rock will slide further down the ice."

At this point I had clearly lost them. They exchanged glances.

"What kind of sport is that?" one asked the other.

"Ah, never mind," I said.

I went to get the hose so we could spray the soapy rugs down.

Greeks! I thought to myself. *How much they miss out on without a good Canadian winter to play in.*

26

KNOT TWENTY-SIX

An Unexpected Prophecy

ONE AFTERNOON SR. NEKTARIA AND I had the task of thoroughly cleaning the guests' dining hall. I was washing the tables while she swept, and we got into a conversation about how she found out about the monastery. She told me her incredible story, a story I found quite representative of the opinion many share towards those they do not understand.

Sr. Nektaria was born and raised in Australia; she is not Greek and has no Greek ancestry. Her mother was of Ukrainian descent, so she and her four siblings were raised as Orthodox Christians. The church they attended in Australia had a mixture of Orthodox nationalities, including Greeks. Growing up, Sr. Nektaria did not have a good opinion of the latter.

"If we got tired during the Divine Liturgy, my mother wouldn't let us sit down. We could only kneel! While the Greek children got to play outside until the Our Father and only then come into the church.

"I hated the way they always dressed up so much for church, the way they seemed to show off. I didn't understand anything then. I didn't understand that when they dressed up they did it because they felt like they were going to see the King.

"I thought they were always blaspheming, saying *Panagia* all the time. I didn't realize that it was because they had true love for the saints and Christ. So they spoke of them with familiarity. In our family home, maybe you would see an icon high up in the corner of the living room, while Greeks had icons everywhere. But I didn't understand them, so I didn't want anything to do with them.

"When I decided to move to Albania for a short work contract, I never considered visiting Greece. A Greek man from my church heard I was moving and wanted to take me out for coffee with him and his wife to speak to me about visiting a monastery in Northern Greece. He wanted me to visit some women's monastery that was only an hour west of Thessaloniki. He said there was another nun there from Australia.

"I didn't want to visit Greece, so I kindly humored him but didn't make any promises. He wrote down the directions to the monastery for me in Greek and insisted on giving me drachmas, the old Greek currency. I tried very hard to refuse them because I knew if I took them I'd be obliged to go.

"'If you can stay there for two to three weeks it will be enough time for you,' he told me. 'No, no, you need about four weeks. Hmm, if you stay five to six weeks I'm certain it will be enough time for you.' After saying this he gave me Abbess Thaisia's book, *Letters to a Young Nun*. When his wife saw this she became upset with him. 'How dare you be so presumptuous, assuming she'll become a nun!' she scolded him.

"I had never considered becoming a nun. I was a regular young adult who didn't live any form of a spiritual life. His comments came completely out of nowhere. I sang in the choir, but I showed no signs of being spiritual in any other way. I took his directions to the monastery, the drachmas, and the book, but was not pleased about it all.

"Since I had a good job in Australia, I had saved a lot of money. Before leaving for Albania, I thought I better set some things up with my bank so that if anything happened to me, my family could access my savings. So I signed everything over to my sister.

"Once I was in Albania, I took out a map and was surprised to see how close I was to the monastery the man wanted me to visit. I really didn't want to return to Australia with the drachmas he gave me and have to tell him I didn't go. So I decided to give in and go to Greece. He told me once I arrived at the monastery to simply ask for Sr. Epomoni.

"After taking a bus to the nearby village and a taxi to the monastery, I arrived in the afternoon and immediately asked for Sr. Epomoni. To my great surprise, it was my catechism teacher from when I was a child! I had no idea she had become a nun. She was as surprised to see me as I was to see her. She spoke to Gerontissa, and they invited me to stay for a week.

"Friday came and Gerontissa asked me when I was leaving. I asked to stay until Monday. On Monday I asked to stay until Friday, and it went on like this for a few weeks. Finally, I told Sr. Epomoni that I wanted to remain close to the monastery. So the nuns had some friends set up a job for me in Thessaloniki.

"The night before I was to leave the monastery, while walking in the courtyard with Sr. Epomoni I told her, 'I really don't want to go to Thessaloniki. I just feel like staying at the monastery.'

"'I think it's time we went and you confessed to Gerontissa,' she told me.

"So, that's what we did. I told Gerontissa everything I ever did in my life—which was extremely difficult and embarrassing to do through a translator—and they had a hieromonk come so I could confess to him and receive absolution.

"Gerontissa agreed to let me stay, and that is when I realized I had been at the monastery for exactly five and a half weeks.

"After hating Greeks my whole life, they became the ones that saved me!" she said, wiping tears from her cheeks.

The Evil Eye

THE CONCEPT OF AN "EVIL EYE" is often misunderstood. Although the Orthodox Church believes the evil eye exists and does harm, it *does not* believe in the "blue eye" as a form of protection—pendants of which are unfortunately sold all over Greece and Turkey. The Church dismisses the practice of wearing or owning a blue eye pendant as superstitious and lacking any power to protect against evil. However, the concept of the evil eye has a legitimate source; it is taken from the Holy Scriptures.

In the Gospel of St. Mark, Christ tells us, "For from within, out of the heart of men, proceed evil thoughts, adulteries, fornications, murders, thefts, covetousness, wickedness, deceit, lewdness, **an evil eye**, blasphemy, pride, foolishness. All these evil things come from within and defile a man" (Mark 7:21–23, emphasis mine).

The evil eye is primarily connected with envy. It is an ill will we exhibit toward someone or something because we are envious. It may be, as many sins are, unintentional at times but can cause harm regardless. The only sure way to protect oneself against the evil eye is first and foremost by communing often, thoroughly confessing, completing one's prayer rule *every* day, and doing obedience to one's spiritual father. In this way one is "covered" by his or her spiritual father's *epitrachelion** (stole), as I have heard the nuns say. However, sometimes God permits us to be affected by the sins of others for reasons only He knows.

Elder Porphyrios speaks about the result of the evil eye, even when it's unintentional, in his book, *Wounded by Love*. He tells a story about a woman who went to visit her friend and saw a beautiful Japanese vase her friend kept in her living room. The next day the woman vividly and passionately told her husband all about how wonderful her friend's vase was. The exact moment at which the woman was telling her husband about the vase, the vase—in her friend's home—cracked and broke into many pieces. "She didn't realize that she had jealousy within her. That was envy, jealousy, evil bewitchment. The evil power can be transmitted, however far apart we are. This is a mystery. Distance is irrelevant. That's why the vase broke," the elder remarks in his book.[12]

The evil eye has caused a few problems at the monastery as well. This is why if I commented that something was beautiful or looked with a lot of wonderment at something, the nuns would tell me, "Make the sign of the cross over it."

At first I thought that was a bit over the top. I felt they were overdoing it, since I thought if I didn't intend to have ill will, or if I didn't know I was envious, nothing bad could come from my exclamations of praise. Although the harm that comes from envious eyes does not exactly originate from the envious *person*, the result is nevertheless harmful. In his homily *Concerning Envy*, St. Basil the Great explains it in this way:

Some think that envious persons bring bad luck merely by a glance. . . . I reject these tales as popular fancies and old wives' gossip. But I do say: the devils, who are enemies of all that is good, use for their own ends such free acts as they find congenial to their wishes. In this way, they make even the eyes of envious persons serviceable to their own purposes.[13]

If we are envious, even in the smallest aspect of our thoughts or words, even while praising something or someone, the evil one will, can, and does take advantage of those sentiments if they are not entirely pure. After hearing the following stories, my acceptance of the Fathers' teachings on the evil eye was merely reaffirmed.

EVERY TWO WEEKS THE SISTERS bake a dozen or so prosphora loaves. They mix the ingredients, work the dough into cylindrical shapes, press them with the seal, and leave them to rise. Once they have risen, they are baked in the oven, and afterward left out to cool.

One particular day a visiting woman, passing through the kitchen, stopped to admire the freshly cooked prosphora. "These prosphora are amazing. The seal came out so well on all of them and there are no cracks. My prosphora don't come out this well."

The next time the sisters made prosphora, they were dismayed to see not one loaf of the whole batch rose properly. They began again. And again the dough wouldn't rise. Finally, they went to Gerontissa and explained their dilemma. She advised them to have the priest read prayers for the evil eye. Following the priest's intercession, the sisters were able to successfully make prosphora again.

SR. SERAPHIMA WAS WATERING the flowers in the courtyard one day, and a young lady from the village was watching her. Suddenly the sister's foot got caught in the hose and she tripped, tumbling to the ground. Seeing the young lady looking at her, she asked, "Galina, what were you just thinking about?"

"I was thinking about what a good nun you are and how hard you work," the young lady responded.

"Try not to think anything," the sister advised her.

THE EVIL ONE LOOKS for every opportunity he can to "put his foot in," as they say in Greek. I know these stories may seem incredible or mere coincidences. Perhaps they are. However, the belief that our internal sins affect those around us is an Orthodox teaching. Our thoughts determine our lives, Elder Thaddeus of Serbia taught.

Our thoughts have a lot of power, and this is the primary reason we struggle to combat and conquer them—for they can harm not only ourselves, but others also. And so, with the divine Psalmist, we pray, "From my secret sins cleanse me, and from those of others spare Thy servant" (Ps. 18:12 LXX).

O Death, Where is Thy Sting?

THE SISTERS KNEW A WOMAN who was a nominal Christian. Her son had slowly developed some bad habits. He became so engrossed in his computer games that gradually his parents saw less of him as he spent more and more time alone in his bedroom playing games. His general disposition grew sour. His parents became concerned, but didn't know what to do.

At some point the young man became ill, and medical examinations revealed he had an aggressive form of cancer. He was admitted to the hospital and shared his room with another young man, ill like himself.

"Don't worry, son, we're going to pay for the best cancer treatments, and you'll become well again!" his mother promised him.

"No, Mama, I'm too far gone. Give the money you would have spent on my treatment to that young man," he said, gesturing to the young man in the next bed. "He will live."

His mother was speechless, but seeing her son's slow but sure transformation into a loving, considerate young man, she understood that his illness had had a positive effect on him. During the time he had left to live, his whole character changed, and he ceased being the strange, selfish person he had become.

On Holy Thursday, the day before we celebrate the Lord's Passion, this woman's son died. She came to the monastery, and entering the church while the service was being conducted, she started shouting, "My child! My child! He died! He's dead!"

The sisters didn't know what to say. Approaching her at the end of the service, they all felt perplexed as to how to offer her comfort.

"On Holy Thursday! On Holy Thursday, sisters! The Lord took him!" she said, with so much joy that, as Sr. Xenia later told me, "You would have thought it was Pascha the way she was speaking. It was like she was experiencing the joy of Pascha!"

KNOT TWENTY-SEVEN

Ora et Labora

DURING THE DAYS LEADING UP to the feast of the monastery's patron saint, I had rarely known such physical exhaustion, oddly accompanied by mental clarity. Days before the feast, I was making a coffee in the kitchen while reflecting on this to Sr. Xenia and Sr. Christodora.

"Yesterday we were so busy I didn't even have time to think. I only noticed it when I entered the church last night for vigil. I thought, *Finally I can think*. And immediately I realized the purpose of manual work—to free the mind from thoughts.

"Many thoughts intrude into my mind during services, but when I am working I just don't have time to think. Now all I need to do is learn the Prayer so that while I work my mind, free from thoughts, will focus on Christ."

"That's it, exactly! The purpose is to weaken the flesh and focus the mind!" Sr. Christodora said.

Protection from My Own Carelessness

AFTER MIDNIGHT, ON THE EVE of the patron saint's feast day, I was still in the church with Sr. Akakia, Sr. Thekla, and Sr. Arsenia. The constant stream of pilgrims coming to venerate had finally slowed down, and we needed to tidy up in order to have the church prepared for Matins and the Divine Liturgy at seven the next morning.

Initially, Sr. Arsenia said we wouldn't mop the floors (since we had done them that morning). Instead, we would just wipe down the stasidia and tidy up the sanctuary. I grabbed a cloth, a bucket of water, and a drying cloth and began wiping down the stasidia while the nuns tidied up other parts of the church. Then, to my dismay, Sr. Arsenia changed her mind about mopping.

"But we'll only wash the floors twice," she kindly condescended.

Off Sr. Thekla and I went to prepare the buckets: one with soapy water, one with clear water. We called this "two hands," meaning one of us would wash the floor once with soapy water while the other—"the second hand"—followed with clear water. I was completely exhausted, because we had been running around for days preparing for the feast day, and apparently my fatigue was obvious.

"We've figured you out: after one week of work at the monastery you're done in," Sr. Thekla told me, smiling.

While I was in the church's nave washing the floor, Sr. Thekla was finishing up part of the narthex. I was close to the bishop's throne and was not being as careful as I ought to have been. As I turned to wash the floor closer to the throne, to my horror, I hit the large microphone they had set up for the feast day.

I watched as it fell in what seemed slow motion. I was completely mortified, fearing it would break—or at least be damaged—if it hit the marble floor. Just as it was about five inches from the ground I caught it, and it didn't suffer any damage. I nearly had a heart attack, but, having righted the microphone, I went over to the icon of the patron saint and bowed low in thanksgiving. I kissed him and said, "Thank you so much!"

I had often envisioned making some sort of big mistake like that while working at the monastery. Every time such a thought would come, I would ask the saint to protect me. I'm thankful that time he did.

A Deceiver yet True

GERONTISSA PHILARETI WAS GOOD AT hiding her spiritual insight (at least from anyone outside the sisterhood). She often avoided speaking and was careful in giving advice. It was clear she would rather fatten you up than make herself a prophet. This was just her character. I have met other abbesses who were entirely different—ones that did not hide their holiness as well as Gerontissa Philareti did. It seemed her own policy was to instruct and love in silence. Her affection and concern for our spiritual health came through when she would cross us with her intricately carved wooden cross. But when I would ask her to instruct me on spiritual matters, she would often respond with, "Ask your spiritual father about that."

I remember once a group of us visited the monastery, and when we were leaving, we went to take her blessing. She had thought we were leaving the next day and was disappointed she wouldn't have the chance to sit and chat with us.

"Then give us a spiritual word!" I said, taking advantage of the opportunity.

"A spiritual word!" she said, laughing.

And without missing a beat she said, "What food can I send home with you?"

She was forever sending food home with us. I can't count the number of times she got the nuns to cook us fish the very day we were leaving so we would have a meal all ready for us when we got home. She loved giving people things, especially food.

"Don't ask Gerontissa for spiritual advice, 'cause she'll load you up with more food than you can carry home!" John would jokingly advise friends.

Some things, however, she could not hide. For instance, like many spiritual people, she was fragrant. I noticed her clothes (and Sr. Paisia's too) always smelt especially wonderful, but I often dismissed this, thinking it was merely the fabric softener the nuns used. I found it strange the other nuns didn't smell the same way, but I didn't realize the sweet smell came from prayer until Sr. Thekla pointed it out to me once.

"Even when Gerontissa's clothes are dirty, they still smell like this. It's from the Prayer."

To see her cooking in the kitchen, sleeves rolled up to her elbows, alongside the other nuns, you would just think she was like everyone else. Her shyness toward spiritually advising people, unless really pushed for help, added to this impression. But her prayer life went much deeper than an ordinary Christian's and resulted in many spiritual gifts. In fact, she was anything but ordinary.

Sr. Theonifi told me about one of the sisterhood's *synaxes** at which Gerontissa shared some very intimate things. They were all sitting together in the gathering room located in the midst of their cells. This room was rather large with benches lining the walls, and traditional Greek embroidered rug-like tapestries hung above each bench as a type of cushioned back.

Sr. Theonifi said, "We were all sitting together on the benches listening attentively to Gerontissa, and she told us, 'Before I leave my cell each morning, I know the state each of you is in. I know how each of you is feeling and what your struggles are. Right now I can see a demon whispering in one sister's ear. I can see another one on a sister's back. And I want you to know that whatever temptations you have, whatever struggles, I have them too, all of them. Everything you go through, I go through with you,' she told us."

Sr. Agathi told me she received great spiritual comfort by merely being in Gerontissa's presence. Many times when she was battling bad thoughts, they would suddenly disperse. Turning around, she would see Gerontissa had come into the room.

DURING THE FIRST THREE DAYS of Great Lent, the nuns all stay in their cells praying and fasting from all food and drink. They also practice fasting from speech so as not to hinder each other's prayers. During this time they only speak when strictly necessary.

Once, during the "three-day," as Greeks call it, Sr. Akakia was doing her prayers in the hallway. Since she and some other sisters shared cells, they would sometimes do their prayers wherever they found an unoccupied place. This way they could have a little privacy.

Praying at the end of the hallway, Sr. Akakia saw Yia-yia, healthy at that time, walk toward Gerontissa's cell and raise her hand to knock on the door. She didn't knock, however, but returned to her cell, most likely not wanting to disturb Gerontissa's silence.

Just then, down the hall near where Sr. Akakia was praying, the phone rang.

"*Evlogeite!** [Bless!]*" Sr. Akakia answered.

"*O Kyrios!*" Gerontissa responded (meaning, "The Lord blesses!").

"Akakia, what did Yia-yia want?" Gerontissa asked.

Sr. Akakia's mouth dropped open. "I—I don't know, Gerontissa," she answered.

Sr. Akakia emphasized to me that Yia-yia did not knock on the door, and that Gerontissa had no way of knowing someone had approached her door, let alone that it was Yia-yia.

OFTEN WE FEEL A CERTAIN connection with a particular saint or angel. Elder Paisios had a close connection with St. Euphemia, Elder Iakovos Tsilikis with St. David the Righteous of Evia, and St. John Chrysostom with St. Paul the Apostle. Gerontissa Philareti had such a connection with St. Nektarios of Pentapolis. She often kept his relics with her.

Michael and Mary, who are close friends with both Sr. Sarah and me, suffered the hardship of having a very ill baby. The baby had a problem with her kidneys and was hospitalized when she was just eight months old. Since Gerontissa was in Thessaloniki the day Sr. Sarah found out, she called her with the troubling news: "Gerontissa, wherever you are, please cross the baby with St. Nektarios's relics."

Later that day, Sr. Sarah spoke with Michael, and he said the baby's fever eased up in the afternoon. When Sr. Sarah found out what time this happened, she realized it was right around the same time she had spoken with Gerontissa.

ONCE, A CARLOAD OF US drove out to the monastery for an afternoon visit. It was close to lunchtime and we were going to leave, but Gerontissa told us to stay for lunch. When Gerontissa tells you to sit and eat, you're hard pressed to refuse her.

While I was visiting the sisters in the kitchen, I saw they were making fish soup. It was a Saturday, and I was the only one in the carload fasting for Holy Communion.[14] But before I managed to tell Sr. Xenia I was fasting, she said, "Constantina, Gerontissa told me to make pasta for you."

I was pleased because I knew they make a fasting sauce for it. I had just assumed that Gerontissa was going to serve us all pasta, since they probably didn't make enough fish soup. To my surprise, Gerontissa served fish soup to everyone else, and pasta only to me, without so much as a comment.

A YOUNG TEENAGER NAMED PHOTINI was visiting from Cyprus once. Her father was Cypriot and her mother was British. She had been struggling with some things—as many young people do—and so Gerontissa, knowing the family well, suggested she spend some time at the monastery over her summer break.

During her visit, Photini wanted to confess some things, so Gerontissa made time to speak with her. (It is common for someone to confess to an abbess in order to seek spiritual advice. An abbess is a type of spiritual parent who, although she does not possess the priesthood and cannot give absolution, is recognized as having the gift of discernment and thus being able to help many people.)

However, when Photini sat down with Gerontissa, she was left speechless. As she prepared to confess, Gerontissa instead told her what she saw before her: Photini's past.

"I just cried while Gerontissa told me all the things I've done since I was young," Photini told me the next day while we prepared strawberries for jam.

She narrated the whole event to me the next morning. "Gerontissa told me not to be sad, but to receive it as a gift. She said she could not see whatever she wanted, but that God gave her the ability in that moment to see my past in order to help me."

Needless to say, Photini was rather shaken up by the event and very remorseful over some mistakes she made in her past. She completely came out of her shell after this. She was only fourteen years old, and you would have thought she was eighteen. It was as if she suddenly stopped being childish and resolved to be more responsible and thoughtful about her actions. The change was visible.

THERE WERE TIMES WHEN GERONTISSA simply couldn't hide her spiritual gifts. She didn't show them off, but used them for the spiritual benefit of those around her. She walked around speaking softly, putting more food on your plate, and making sure you never left without a freshly baked loaf of bread—but if you sought a sign, she hindered you from receiving one. If you simply approached her as an ordinary nun cooking you pasta, you missed the opportunity to see her spiritual intuition.

KNOT TWENTY-EIGHT

Mavroudis the Martyr

KALLIOPI LIVED IN THE VILLAGE nearest the monastery. I met her for the first time when we both visited the monastery to help the sisters with the olives from their orchard. As we sorted olives together, we began a conversation about new martyrs. I asked her if there were any martyrs among the local saints. Kalliopi mentioned Mavroudis, a martyr who had lived in her father's town. Mavroudis's martyrdom is recounted in a folk song written by the locals, which she sang for us.

Similar to Byzantine chant, some older Greek folk songs have a haunting feel to them. I found some to be quite melancholic. They never reminded me of our Atlantic Canadian folk songs—some of which are sailors' songs, making light of hardships. Many Greek folk songs cause suffering and longing experienced long ago to come back and settle in your chest.

The song Kalliopi sang to us explains how Mavroudis was killed by Muslim Turks for refusing to denounce his Christian faith and embrace Islam. He had an argument with some Turks and insulted their faith. So the Turks threatened to throw him into the fire if he didn't agree to become a "Turk"—in other words, a Muslim. He asked them to give him some time to make up his mind, and they granted him permission.

On seeing his mother approach, he asked her, "Mama, what shall I do? They want me to become a Turk or they will throw me into the fire."

"Better to be a Turk and live, than dead in the fire!" she advised him.

He was very sorrowful when he heard her answer in this way, and crying and pulling his hair he said to her, "No, I will wait for my love to come and tell me what she thinks."

He waited, and when his wife arrived he asked her, "Tell me, my love, should I become a Turk or be thrown into the fire?"

"It's better for you to enter the fire than to become a Muslim," she answered. On hearing this, the Turks threw them both into the fire, granting them a martyr's death.

The song ends, "Like candles they burned; like incense they smelt. Doves they became; to the heavens they flew."

There were, of course, a few wet cheeks by the time Kalliopi finished singing.

Things Aren't Always As They Appear

GERONTISSA HAS TWO NEPHEWS who are Navy Seals. They are both extremely handsome, with wonderful personalities to match. Once I was visiting while one of the nephews was there with his wife and child. When they were leaving, he came into the kitchen to say goodbye. He hugged and—in keeping with the Greek custom—kissed everyone. I strategically stayed behind the island in the kitchen trying to avoid having to say goodbye to him. I mentioned this to Sr. Sarah, adding that, if I were a nun, I would have felt very uncomfortable having to hug and kiss him, since I felt this way even as a layperson.

She told me she had the same reaction the first few times she met Gerontissa's nephews. She confided in another sister about how she felt, and that sister shared the following story with her.

Years earlier she had also had the same difficulty and mentioned it to Gerontissa. Gerontissa's answer to her was, "I don't worry about the nun who hugs and kisses men without being uncomfortable. It's the nun who walks around not being able to look up at a man that you need to worry about."

Obviously she said this both to help and humble the sister. But nevertheless, it's a good lesson to be careful with the conclusions we draw about others, because our opinion about the intentions behind another's action may not correspond with reality.

He Exalts Them of Low Degree

I'LL SHARE WITH YOU YET another experience I had with the blind Elder Isidoros of the Holy Mountain. This servant of God was so humble that although he worked many miracles—such as curing people of cancer, healing others of multiple sclerosis, curing a blind woman—he believed none of it came as a result of his own holiness. He felt the miracles happened solely through the prayers of his spiritual father, Elder Ephraim of St. Anthony's Monastery in Arizona.

By the time I met him, Elder Isidoros had been a spiritual child of

Elder Ephraim for over thirty years. He had a thirty-three-knot prayer rope (the kind worn on the wrist) given to him by Elder Ephraim, which he kept in a small clear plastic bag with an icon of the Mother of God the Sweet-kisser (housed in Philotheou Monastery) taped onto it. With this simple, small prayer rope he prayed over people, and they were healed from all sorts of ailments. He attributed it all to the prayers of his spiritual father.

"Through the prayers of my Geronda," he would say. And just like that, miracles happened!

By his profound humility, strong faith, and pure heart he attracted the grace of God, and God worked miracles through him. Because he thought himself unworthy to do such miracles, God enabled him to work them.

Christ tells us, "If you had faith as a grain of mustard . . ." (Luke 17:6). This faith he obviously had.

A presvytera who lived quite close to the monastery had been diagnosed with breast cancer. She and her husband had four children. From his grief and worry that their children would lose their mother, the priest became paler each day. The weight of his wife's impending death hung around his neck like a millstone. A friend of theirs told them Elder Isidoros was at the monastery. She suggested they go and take his blessing, and perhaps he could pray over the presvytera. They wisely heeded her advice and came to the monastery while I was also there.

When they went in to see the elder, he greeted them. They spoke a little, and he took out the relics he always carried around with him and offered them for veneration. Then he took out his little plastic bag with the small prayer rope inside and laid it on her.

"Through the prayers of Geronda Ephraim," he said. And then in his characteristically strange, but funny way he said, "It's leaving, it's leaving! The cat will eat it!"

And that was it; his faith had healed her.

His spiritual daughter, a friend of mine, told me afterward that whenever someone he prayed over came to him to tell him the doctors could no longer locate the cancer, he always responded, "Yeah, because the cat ate it!"

During this same visit, my eczema was very bad, especially on my hands. The sisters told me to ask the elder to pray over them, so I took the opportunity while he was sitting with me when I was measuring and packaging some pasta.

"Papouli, I have really bad eczema on my hands right now, and they hurt a lot. Do you think you can pray over them?"

He took out the small prayer rope from his pocket and placed it in between my hands so that the eczema rashes were touching the plastic bag that held the rope. With my hands like this, he held them in his own.

"Papou, Geronda, do something!" he said, in the same way a child speaks to his father. He began to pray fervently, *"Kyrie Isou Hriste eleison me . . . Lord Jesus Christ, have mercy on me."* He said *"Papou"* signifying Elder Joseph the Hesychast, his spiritual "grandfather," the spiritual father of Elder Ephraim, and "Geronda," obviously, addressing Elder Ephraim.

"How do you feel?" he asked me. "Do you feel warmth?"

"Mostly in my face, Geronda, but I think it's because I'm a little embarrassed," I said.

He continued to pray fervently.

"And now? Now, how do you feel?" he asked.

I began to have a strong feeling of spiritual joy in my heart.

"I feel joy," I said.

"Joy? Anything else?" he asked.

"And peace."

He continued to pray, and I continued to feel spiritually energized.

It was as though he were an outlet and my hands were the plug. I plugged into the spiritual outlet, and spiritual joy and peace were traveling through his hands into mine and through my whole body, right down into my feet, like an electrical current.

"Joy and peace, is that it?"

"A lot of peace," I said quietly.

"And your hands, how do they feel?" he asked, letting them go.

I looked at them. The rashes were still there, but the sensation I was feeling overwhelmed any hint of irritation I had felt just a few moments ago.

"Better," I said.

I felt so peaceful, so full of spiritual joy, that I had no other answer to give. Through his humble prayer, he allowed those spiritual sensations to pass from him into me. I felt spiritually rejuvenated for at least three days following this encounter. When I returned home, I put some ointment on my hands, and the rashes disappeared. I have not had any eczema rashes return since that time, even though I've had eczema since I was a teenager.

I must confess, however, that the spiritual peace and joy the elder conducted into me mean more to me than having some rashes healed. God knows what we need. The eczema may return, and I may have to live with that condition. But recalling and maintaining the spiritual fruit the elder offered me would be a far greater miracle. Through his prayers and his humble example, I hope to someday re-establish those spiritual sentiments and have them remain in my heart for the rest of my life.

From this experience I learned that when God gives us these small spiritual boosts, we should struggle with all our might to safeguard them with prayer and watchfulness. For they may well go away, with or without negligence, but it's always better if we do all we can to keep them.

Even recalling the story fills me with courage to struggle harder. Ultimately this is what miracles should do for us. This is what my encounter with the elder taught me. Miracles are opportunities for our faith to increase and our resolve to struggle harder to be strengthened. God is glorified by His saints, and He glorifies them!

29

KNOT TWENTY-NINE

Obedience: The Source of Eternal Salvation (Heb. 5:9)

LATE ONE EVENING WHILE SR. THEKLA, Sr. Sarah, and I were looking at some photos of my sketches and icons, Sr. Thekla told us, "I once drew a picture of Elder Philotheos Zervakos from a photograph I had. I was in my cell reading and, after looking at his photo, I just felt like drawing. So I picked up a pencil and a scrap piece of paper and drew his portrait. It turned out really well. I had never drawn something so well before. It was by far the best piece I had ever done.

"So I decided to show it to Gerontissa. I went to her and handed her my drawing of the elder. She took it and looked at me.

"'Who gave you a blessing to draw that?' she asked me.

"'*Evlogisan,** Gerontissa. No one gave me a blessing,' I answered her.

"'Burn it,' she said, handing it back to me.

"'May it be blessed,' I said and immediately threw it into the fire," Sr. Thekla said, finishing her story.

"Why did Gerontissa tell you to do that?" I asked.

"Because I didn't have a blessing, and you never know what the evil one will do if you do things without a blessing. He is always looking for a way in, and it's best for us not to give him one."

"Were you upset?" I asked.

"No. I drew the elder and it was very good, but since I didn't have a blessing, it didn't matter to me that I had to burn it."

"Wow," I said. "I remember Elder Porphyrios describes a similar thing that happened to him. Do you remember?"

"Didn't he carve something out of wood without a blessing?" Sr. Sarah asked.

"Yeah, he carved a bird with grapes, and when his elder came home and saw it, he smashed it to bits," I told them.

"That's right, I remember reading that. Well, it's not a good idea for us to do things without a blessing," Sr. Thekla responded.

A Monastic's Handicraft

ALONG WITH ALL THE REGULAR TASKS of maintaining and restoring a monastery, the nuns also did some beautiful handicrafts: they painted icons and embroidered ecclesiastical garments, among other things.

Sr. Xenia and Sr. Seraphima had taken a course on embroidery a few years back, so they tried to put their talent to good use whenever they found the time. However, because they had so much other, more pressing, work, they hardly ever had the opportunity to embroider. The only time they seemed to find was in the middle of the night, and even then this came only during winter. So occasionally during the dark winter nights a faint light would shine out from the top floor of the workrooms.

Among the things the sisters learned to embroider were icons, and they did an exquisite job. One afternoon Sr. Xenia showed me their work. Sr. Seraphima learned how to embroider faces, while Sr. Xenia embroidered garments. Together they had done an icon of Christ enthroned, a few seraphim and cherubim, and a most beautiful icon of St. Katherine the Great Martyr, complete with the spiked wheel.

Occasionally they took orders to make altar cloths but, because they had so many other things they had to attend to, it took an exceptionally long time to complete them. Over the years, they had, however, managed to embroider a good number of pieces. One afternoon Sr. Xenia showed me the photo album of all their work. One of the photos was of Gerontissa's schema.

Quite a few years earlier Sr. Seraphima, with the help of an older nun, embroidered Gerontissa's analavos, her schema garment. The Greek word *analavos* means "to take on" or "to bear," in this instance signifying the taking up of the cross (Luke 9:23) by the great-schema monk or nun. Tonsure into the great schema is the highest grade of Orthodox monasticism. The only difference between schema garments in the various Orthodox jurisdictions is the style. Unlike in the Russian tradition (and some others), the Greek schema does not include a hood, but rather consists only of the garment (the analavos) worn around the neck, which covers the front and reaches down past the knees. It looks similar to a priest's stole and in the Greek tradition is embroidered in color, predominantly red.

In the photo of Gerontissa's schema, I could see that the sisters embroidered the cross and all the traditional symbols that accompany the cross (1 Corinthians 1:18). On many schemas there is a rooster to remind us of St. Peter's denial (Matt. 26:74), a plaque at the foot of the cross to remind us of Christ's "footstool" (Ps. 131:7), a reed to remind us of the hyssop He was given to drink (John 19:19–20), a lance signifying the wound He received (John 19:34), a ladder by which St. Joseph of Arimathea took down His holy body (Matt. 27:57), and many other symbols associated with Christ's passion.

Gerontissa's schema also had the traditional abbreviations that extol the cross as the power of God. For example, the initials ΞΓΘΗ, which mean, "The tasting of the tree brought about death"; ΣΞΖΕ: "Through the Tree of the Cross have we found Life"; and ΤΤΔΦ: "Honored trophy, the dread of demons." The only unique item the nuns added to Gerontissa's schema was the embroidered words of the cherubic hymn of Holy Saturday. They put this script around the frame of the schema: "Let all mortal flesh keep silence and stand with fear and trembling; and let it take no thought for any earthly thing."

The other magnificent handicraft the sisters did that impressed me immensely was decorating Paschal candles. Sr. Paisia had a real talent for being creative. So the sisters had a lot of glass and plastic beads for her crafts. Every year, just before Pascha, she would embed beads in large, pure beeswax candles to give away as blessings for Pascha. She would make two for the local bishop and two for their spiritual father so they could hold them during the singing of "Come receive the Light" on Holy Saturday night. She also made a smaller one for Gerontissa as her Paschal candle.

I took great delight in looking through the photo album of all her past Paschal candles. The most remarkable aspect was the symmetry. She did swirls and designs in all sorts of colors and combinations, but from top to bottom the symmetry was precise. For the focal point of the candle she would place a miniature icon of the Resurrection or make a cross out of beads.

This was the work of these Greek nuns: careful, exact, beautiful, and meaningful. From thoroughly cleaning the monastery once a week, to regularly washing the ceilings, to making sure to cut a small cross in each loaf of bread they baked, they were meticulous. They overlooked nothing and perfected every detail.

The principle behind monastic precision is similar to the one encountered in the military. By having all the small things in order, tidy and ready, they are able to keep order and exactitude in battle. In fact, the monastery has much in common with the military. In both, complete obedience is expected. In both, watchfulness is cultivated. And in both, people willingly enlist, knowing they may come face to face with death. In fact, in the case of monasticism, facing death to one's own will is guaranteed if one is to complete his or her mission successfully.

All Christians are soldiers, enlisted to fight against the enemy of man's salvation. Monastics are one step above—they are the "Special Forces." But regardless of rank, we should all fight in unity and ceaselessly, with order and precision, so that we might find victory.

Patience in Suffering Is Greatly Rewarded

AS I MENTIONED EARLIER, when Sr. Markella was twelve years old, she was sent to work for a family because her own was too poor to support her. She lived with a wealthier family that had two children, and she did all the chores. Though she was a young girl, Sr. Markella was stocky, so her boss—the man of the house—would call her "George" instead of Georgia, which was her name in the world.

One night he told little "George" to turn the lights off. When she reached up to turn the switch off, she was electrocuted. The family rushed her to the village's doctor, but it was no use. She completely lost the use of her right arm. For the rest of her life she functioned with the proper use of only her left arm.

"I raised five children with this one arm!" she used to say.

"I did all the chores in the house, hung out the laundry, did everything with one arm. I'll show you how. I would use my good arm to grab my bad arm and lift it up like this. That way I could at least use my fingers," she explained to me once.

She was very joyful and proud of her accomplishments. Raising five children with the use of only one arm is indeed impressive, but being joyful about it is even more so!

She never felt sorry for herself; instead she made full use of her talents. She would even sew clothes for her children, and taught them to do the same. Her daughter, who wanted to become a nun from a young age, would make her own skirts, long and modest. When her daughter left for school, Sr. Markella, who was not so monastic-friendly at that time, would take the newly made skirts and shorten them so they would be more stylish. When her daughter got home, she would simply sew more material back onto her skirts. Despite her best attempts, her modest daughter became an abbess in a monastery in Peloponnesus, and Sr. Markella ultimately became a great-schema nun.

Sr. Akakia, Sr. Markella's cell attendant, told me Sr. Markella also did a lot of charitable works while in the world. She said that was one of the primary reasons, together with how much she suffered, that she experienced so many spiritual things—things like hearing her guardian angel chanting.

One afternoon Sr. Markella was sitting near the fire looking tired, so I sat with her for some time. She was happy to have the company, and since she knew me well by that point, she started telling me some things she experienced.

"Once I was ill and had to go to the hospital. I was there in my hospital bed, and the window was to my left. Suddenly I heard the most exquisite chanting coming from my left—pay attention now, it's important that it was coming from my left! I thought it must be coming from the window, but I couldn't figure out what the source was. When Gerontissa came to visit me, I told her, 'I hear beautiful chanting coming from the window over there.'

"At first Gerontissa told me not to pay attention to it because she wasn't sure if it was a temptation. She called Geronda and asked him about it, and he told her, 'It's to help her have patience because she is about to suffer a lot.'

"That's when Gerontissa told me, 'It's not coming from the window. It's coming from your heart. It's your guardian angel chanting.'

"You see! That's why I thought it was from the window, on my left side! But it was from my heart! Soon afterward I lost the ability to walk and ended up in this wheelchair. But when I feel sad or very ill, I just tell him, 'My angel, sing a little for me,' and he does."

She also had *seen* her guardian angel. And not only him, but also the angel that accompanies her from her tonsure into the great schema. When a monastic takes the great schema, he or she also receives another guardian angel, the same way we all do in Holy Baptism. She described in detail how they dress, the color of their robes, and how her guardian angel's garments differ from the great-schema angel's.

I remember she became very ill for a time and stopped coming out of her cell. She had lost all the enthusiasm she once daily exhibited and could hardly speak. All day and all night the sisters were on a schedule to sit and tend to her. So the next time I came to visit, I went to see her in her cell since she had gotten better.

She was a new person. It was like she had been resurrected from the dead. What a change! She kept telling me how she had thought she was going to die, but that it didn't seem that way now, and how she just wanted to live a little longer.

Many times I have heard it said of a person that his or her face shone, but I never experienced that myself until I saw her that day. She was so full of joy that her face literally looked as though it contained a sort of brightness. She started telling me about some things she thought would happen in my and my husband's future, and Sr. Akakia said, "If Markella says it, it's true."

As I was leaving, I took her right hand and kissed it.

"Come down close so I can kiss your cheeks," she told me.

I left her cell full of joy that her health had been restored. I was not yet ready to say goodbye to my dear Sr. Markella.

KNOT THIRTY

Trial by Fire

ONE DAY, JUST AFTER RECEIVING the blessing of the monastery's spiritual father to become a novice, Sr. Thekla was tending to the wood stove. She had lit the fire as usual, but on returning to check on it, she found the fire had almost completely gone out. She reached in and put more kindling inside. To her horror, her entire left hand became engulfed in flames.

Instead of smothering the fire on her hand, she panicked and ran. She ran down the stairs, out the door, and across the courtyard to where water was pouring out of the fountain. Needless to say, the damage was horrific.

Narrating this story to me years after it had occurred, she told me it was a temptation from the evil one. She said he was angry that she had become a novice. Since receiving the letter from their spiritual father, she had been very excited, and this was the devil's way of displaying his malice and hatred. Thankfully, the damage from the fire miraculously left no scarring. To see her hand today, you would never know it had once been entirely burned by fire.

While Elder Isidoros was staying at the monastery, she also told him this story. He asked for her hand, took out his small prayer rope from Elder Ephraim, and placed it on her hand.

"No, no, Geronda, it's all gone now. That was a long time ago. You can pray over my head instead. It's full of stupid logismoi [thoughts]."

She knelt down and guided his hand so that he placed the prayer rope on her head. I was in the same room with them, so I said, "Well, since you're praying over heads, you might as well pray over mine."

"Come kneel down," he told me.

I knelt beside Sr. Thekla, and he placed one hand on each of us. He kept tapping his finger on our heads.

"What's in here? What's in here?" he teased.

"Nothing," Sr. Thekla said, laughing.

"Sins and passions," I told him.

"Garbage! Garbage!" he teased us. "They're full of garbage!"

While he was knocking on my head—although I knew he was partially playing—I felt as though he were doing it to sort of get rid of all that garbage. I know that doesn't really convey much, but these things are difficult to express. In any case, I would love to have him around so he could "take out the garbage" every time my mind is full of trash!

Chocolate, Loukoumia, and Greek Cookies

THE SISTERS MADE A VARIETY of sweets that they sold in their bookstore. Personally, I enjoyed the monastery's *kourabiedes* cookies the most. Once, when we went over to the bakery to help with something, I noticed a bowl of broken ones left to the side. Since they had broken, the sisters didn't package them with the rest.

I asked to have one, and they told me to take the whole bowl. As we walked back to the guest house, my brother Matthew teased me, "You better make sure Sr. Savina doesn't see you carrying those cookies!"

LEARNING THAT I SHARED HER love of chocolate, Sr. Marina would always try to provide me with a little sweet whenever I was visiting and she was the guest master. One afternoon, just before siesta, she came into my room giggling. She pulled out a handful of chocolates from her pocket and dropped them all on my bed.

EARLY ONE DECEMBER, JOHN AND I received a call from Sr. Sarah telling us that the nuns were all requesting our help with the baking and packaging of their Christmas sweets. Needless to say, neither one of us wanted to refuse helping with sweets. So as soon as our schedules freed up a bit, we arrived ready for work. Morning until evening we were in the bakery with the nuns trying to help them fill all the orders they received.

All year round they make *loukoumia* (Turkish delight—but don't tell Greeks I called it that!) and kourabiedes. But for Christmas they cut the kourabiedes into various festive shapes. They also make *melomakarona* for Christmas, which is a special Greek Christmas cookie, traditionally from Constantinople. They are primarily made with orange juice, cognac, and spices; then they are covered in syrup and sprinkled with crushed walnuts on top. Both the kourabiedes and the melomakarona are fast-friendly, so the faithful can enjoy them in the days leading up to

Christmas. The sisters baked non-stop while we boxed the thousands of cookies they made.

We also helped with the loukoumia. After the batch was ready, we would separate it into different bowls. We would then add the different flavoring to each batch. Their most famous flavor was caramel. And besides the traditional ones, they also had strawberry and banana flavors. After we mixed in the flavoring and added the food coloring, we poured each batch into a separate tray dusted with powdered sugar, and put even more powdered sugar all over the top.

Once they set, Sr. Arsenia would cut them into long strips, the length of the tray. John and I took three of these strips at a time and cut them into one-inch squares, tossed them in more powdered sugar, and then they were ready to be boxed, or just eaten.

After doing this for a few days, all our clothes, and even our hair, started taking on the smell of sugar and syrup. The nuns laughed and told us, "Everyone on the train to Thessaloniki will think you work at a *zaharoplastio* [a sweets bakery]!"

A Blessed Christian Family

AS I SAID ABOVE, Sr. Xenia's mother, a presvytera, was an ascetic in the world. She was also blessed with many spiritual experiences. Sr. Xenia's father was no less pious. When he was a young man, he had a dream in which he saw his future wife and was informed of what her name and surname would be.

While walking home one evening, he literally ran into a young woman. Having knocked her over, he extended his hand to help her up. He asked her name and was flabbergasted to hear her say her name was Christina Markas. Out of utter surprise he yelled, "You're supposed to be my wife!"

Needless to say, she was more than apprehensive and fled. He tried in vain for weeks to see her, but she avoided him. Finally she agreed to see him, and eventually they did indeed get married.

Years later, their eight children all became very ill at the same time. They were all hospitalized and the doctors could not figure out what the problem was, so all the children had to stay in the hospital for days.

They all had high temperatures and exhibited influenza-like symptoms. Late one night, while Presvytera Christina was in the room with the children praying the Supplication service to the Mother of God, a lady dressed as a nun came in carrying a baby. Standing up quickly, Presvytera said, "Please, miss, we don't know why the children are sick, and they may be contagious. Your baby shouldn't be in here!"

But the woman paid no attention to her and walked around the eight children, who were asleep in their beds. And as suddenly as she entered, she exited.

The next morning all the children were as hyper and as energetic as any regular healthy children would be. Their temperatures had all gone down, and they were all insisting, "Mommy, Mommy, let's go home!"

But the doctor refused to allow them to leave. "We do not know what caused the problem, so we cannot let them go regardless of how healthy they seem," he told Presvytera Christina.

The children stayed a few more days, but because they were perfectly healthy and no signs of illness returned, the doctors gave in and let them go home.

A year or so later, Presvytera Christina and her husband went on a pilgrimage to the island of Tinos to venerate that well-known and miraculous icon of the Mother of God, the Great Joy. When Presvytera saw this particular icon of the Most Holy Mother of God, she instantly recognized the lady who had visited her children in the hospital. Having her assumption confirmed by her spiritual father, she glorified God that His Mother had healed her children, four of whom later became monastics.

The Only Thing I Know Is That I Know Nothing

IT WAS A SUMMER EVENING. We had been busy stocking the bookstore when Gerontissa Philareti had Sr. Seraphima come and get me.

This was the first time I had the opportunity to speak with Gerontissa in private. I was nervous, not about what she might say to me, but that I might not be able to understand her. I found her the hardest of all the sisters to understand. She was so soft-spoken that I think I would have strained to understand her in English.

"Here, you might need these," Sr. Sarah said, tossing me a small package of tissues.

"Why?" I asked.

"In case you cry while speaking to Gerontissa. I always used to."

Although I can be emotional, I didn't anticipate crying, and thankfully I didn't. But those tissues were not the only thing to take me by surprise that evening.

I walked across the dimly lit courtyard and looked up at the stars. Living in the city prevented me from seeing all those marvelous little "oil lamps" burning in the heavens before the throne of God.

Gerontissa was sitting in the courtyard, off to the side. Her foot was resting on a small stool and she was holding a long prayer rope with thousands of little knots in her right hand. Standing in front of her, I bent low, and she slightly raised her hand for me to kiss it. She didn't ask me anything. She was silent, waiting for me to speak when I was ready.

I sat down beside her and told her a bit about my family, asked her advice about some things, confided in her about some ongoing temptations, and talked about my spiritual father.

Suddenly and without warning, she said, simply and with no harshness whatsoever, "You have a lot to learn. You know nothing."

I wasn't offended by her words. I understood her to speak without the slightest judgment. She was telling me the truth, not her opinion. I felt this way because, as St. Theophan the Recluse says, her words were spoken in love:

To [correct someone]—there is nothing simpler; but to do it in such a way that it bears fruit is difficult in the extreme. Everything must breathe with the most sincere and zealous love—not only the content of what you say, but even your glance, and expression, and tone of voice. Then it may be hoped that this will achieve its aim. But without this love, it is better not to undertake such a step: it will come out worse, produce the most sorrowful discord.[15]

Her words did, however, take me by surprise. Looking at her wide-eyed, I asked: "Gerontissa, what should I do? Who can I learn from?"

"Visit monasteries, come here," she said casually, shrugging and adjusting her vest.

And that was it. She didn't say any more on the topic. But of course I understood the meaning and purpose of her statement to be twofold. Although she really did speak the truth, I also felt as though her words were meant to humble me. They did the trick, because they have found their way into my thoughts on countless occasions, with the same result each time—confirming that according to a God-bearing mother, I know nothing. Why does my "old self" try to convince me otherwise, whispering that I'm wise and important? The truth has been stated; the only thing left is for me to accept it.

KNOT THIRTY-ONE

Taking a Spiritual Inventory

SINCE SR. SARAH AND I had become such close friends, we relished the few moments we found to sit and talk during my visits. With the hectic workload at the monastery, our conversations were often interrupted with, "Where should I put this?" and "Just wait, I need to go get the pasta out of the dehumidifier."

So when I visited we would occasionally try to catch up after lunch while everyone rested. During one of my favorite visits, though, instead of chatting in the afternoon, we stayed up really late. We sat in the main gallery because I was sharing my room with another visitor and all the other guest rooms were occupied.

Around eleven PM, one by one, all the nuns started heading down to their cells; we took Gerontissa's blessing and continued our conversation. At that time I was going through some things and needed a friend to talk to. Since Sr. Sarah was a nun, it was even more helpful to confide in her.

Something that amazed me about knowing Sr. Sarah for years was how much she spiritually grew in that time. Each visit to the monastery found me that much more impressed by her, more proud of her, more humbled by her. She was like a sunflower; she started off a little seedling, and slowly but surely she grew up out of the earth. In the beginning her stem was thin, needed strengthening—her bud was not yet ready to blossom, but over time she grew.

She grew and became strong through drinking the water of obedience and being nourished by the sun of humility. Like a sunflower turning toward the sun, her face was always turned in the direction of humility. Before I knew it, she had become a towering sunflower, with large, bright petals in full blossom and a stem so thick it would be difficult to break. She had become a seasoned monastic before my eyes, and I was inexpressibly grateful to God for allowing me to witness the growth of His servant. I pray that she continues to blossom until the day she will pass into true life. This is the fruit of a life lived in obedience, prayerfulness, and humility—the fruit of which even we in the world can produce, as we will see in a moment.

During our late-night chat, we spoke about how important it is for us to know ourselves, as well as our daily victories and failures. I told her I had a bad habit of only writing down all the sins, passions, bad thoughts, and oversights I committed—which always resulted in my feeling as though the day were a waste. Whereas writing down the ways in which we at least *attempt* to curb our actions or swallow our bad words both encourages us and reminds us what areas we need improvement in.

So I asked her, "How do we do that? How do we overcome our struggles?"

She did something for me that was beyond helpful, and I will share it with you just as she expressed it to me. However, it comes with a warning, the same humorous warning she gave me: "Don't get scandalized by my petty failures." Having stated this, she proceeded to tell me, in detail, the five ways in which she failed the day before and what she should have done instead.

"First of all, I am about to start my period. I am always weaker, more tired, and more cranky just before I have my period. So I need to be especially watchful during this time. Knowing this, I should have been more watchful and more prayerful before I even left my cell in the morning.

"Second, I was working in the kitchen. This is the hardest and most tiring job. So throughout the day I should have paid more attention to my thoughts. I should have cut them off when they came to mind and been more focused on saying the Jesus Prayer.

"The success or failure of my day wholly depends on whether or not I have controlled my thoughts. If I have allowed my mind to wander, then by the time I go to my cell at night I will feel I did not have a good day.

"At lunchtime Gerontissa told us about a huge temptation that happened while the nuns were working in the garden. It was really bad, and we were all upset about it. At times when I am particularly struggling with something, I excuse myself and go to the chapel of the Dormition and try to recompose myself. Yesterday, when I heard about what happened in the garden, instead of allowing myself to dwell on it and become more upset, I should have gone to the chapel. But I didn't. So that was the third mistake I made.

"The fourth thing happened in the evening when some of the nuns were eating dinner. I grabbed some food and went into the dining hall to eat as well. I sat down and thought, 'I just want fifteen minutes to myself.' But as soon as I started eating, one of the nuns working with me in the kitchen came in and said, 'What are you doing? We have dishes to dry, come help.'

"Instead of saying, 'May it be blessed,' I talked back to her, and because she was also having a difficult day, she responded poorly.

"So I had started a fight because *I* wanted fifteen minutes to myself. I never should have thought I was worthy of having a break and should never have talked back to her. I went and did a *metanoia** (prostration) to her. Then I did one to all the nuns who were in the dining hall during that unpleasant incident.

"The last mistake I made was at the end of the day when I returned to my cell. I shouldn't have allowed myself to sit and cry about the argument I caused. I should have just gone and confessed it to Gerontissa and gotten over it!" She said this last bit quietly laughing.

What Sr. Sarah explained to me was what we call in Greek a *pnevmatiko tameio*, a spiritual inventory—the practice of taking stock of how we spiritually spent our day. It is especially helpful for examining our failures and reflecting on how we should have made them victories.

If only I could be this insightful, this precise about my failures each day, I would be much better equipped to deal with my sins, passions, harmful thoughts, and negative inclinations. Every evening, if I were to sit down and be honest with myself, the way Sr. Sarah was, my confessions would always be thorough and my days better spent.

Greeks Do Not Have Big Noses!

LATE ONE SUMMER NIGHT, Sr. Sarah and I were sitting outside and speaking with Sr. Paisia about some difficulties my husband had recently gone through. The conversation turned to some visitors we had met earlier that day at the monastery. I mentioned that one of the young ladies—they were all from England—was of Greek heritage, and that it was obvious since "she had a big nose."

Boy, was that a mistake! Sr. Paisia slowly turned and looked at me with mouth agape and punched me in the arm. "Greeks *do not* have big noses! People from Pontus do!"

I started laughing uncontrollably while rubbing my arm.

"I didn't mean to be insulting—I just thought it was commonly acknowledged that Greeks have big noses. That's why I always thought everyone, including children, stares at me in Greece. My nose is small, so it's obvious I'm not Greek."

"People stare at you because of the way you dress, not because you have a small nose!" she said, very animated.

"Well, I'm sorry. I was wrong to say Greeks have big noses," I said, still laughing.

Sr. Paisia, as spiritual as she was, could be so funny, but with her you couldn't get away with much. Despite her punches I still loved her, and despite my insults I'm pretty sure she still loved me.

What Shall I Name Thee? I Am in Doubt and Stand in Awe!

THE LOVE AND ADMIRATION THE saints have for the Most Holy Theotokos is one of the main common characteristics of their holiness. Countless are the stories in which you read of the saints' devotion to the All-holy Lady. St. Mary of Egypt went to live out her days in the desert after her encounter with an icon of the Mother of God. St.

Nektarios wrote hymns to her in Ancient Greek to demonstrate his love and devotion to her. And Elder Joseph the Hesychast could barely say her name without tears streaming down his face.

Elder Isidoros the blind was also like that. One evening, sitting down with a group of people, he bowed his head and crossed himself while tears rolled down his cheeks. Wiping them away, he said, "Excuse me, but at this time of night the love of the Mother of God pulls me."

"That's why," the nuns told me, "he won't speak about Panagia in front of too many people. He'll start to cry."

One afternoon I sat with the elder in the reception room. Since we were alone, I thought I'd take the opportunity to start up the conversation about the Mother of God he had said we would have.

"Papouli, why don't you talk to me about Panagia now?"

"Okay, what you would like to know?"

"Why don't you just tell me about her?" I asked him.

"She is . . . she is . . ." he said, raising his hand in the air and waving it in a circular motion—a gesture Greeks do when they are either pleased or annoyed about something.

"She is . . . she is . . . she's like . . ." he said, rubbing his hands together and ever so slightly smiling.

"I can't describe her. She's indescribable!" he finally said.

He then started singing the Supplicatory Canon to her: "Now to God's Mother let us humble sinners run in haste and in repentance let us fall down before her feet, crying aloud with fervor from the depths of our souls, 'Sovereign Lady, help us now, have compassion upon us, hasten for we perish from our many offenses. Let not your servants go empty away; we have you as our only hope.'"

"Do you have the *Paraclesis** here?" the elder asked.

"Yes, Papouli, but it's in English," I told him.

"Ah, never mind," he said. He leaned his head back and rested it against the wall.

"How can we become like her?" I asked.

"You know she lived in the Temple from the age of three on," he said.

"Yes, I know. She was the first hesychast."

"That's right! That's right!" he said. "She was the most pure person that ever lived. She was pure because she never once accepted a bad thought. Not once. She kept her mind, her soul, and her body perfectly pure."

I understood this to be his answer to my question. We can become like her if we also control our thoughts and struggle to attain purity of heart and mind.

He sang some different hymns to her and then he told me, "The more we cry out to her, the more she will harken to our prayers."

I knew he spoke from experience. For, although he was blind since birth, when he went to the Holy Mountain to become a monk, his sight was gradually restored. For ten days he could see, but he told the Mother of God, "Panagia, take my sight back so I don't lose Paradise."

And she did.

But he wasn't truly blind. He simply couldn't use his bodily eyes. He's been known to describe things in detail, things he couldn't possibly know if he were *truly* blind. "And Jesus said, 'For judgment I have come into this world, that those who do not see may see, and that those who see may be made blind'" (John 9:39).

32

KNOT THIRTY-TWO

Worse Than All

THE NUNS NEVER CONSIDERED their personal lives to be any more spiritual than the lives of Christians in the world. They looked at us in the world as though we were examples for them and not the other way around.

The sisters were always so impressed by this or that person's good works. They were always feeling sympathy for those that suffered loss and hardship. They were humbled when people in the world asked questions about leading spiritual lives. And they were always impressed by the ascetical practices and prayer lives of their fellow Christians.

The nuns always had a lot of love for everyone. They were also quite innocent. So while they were genuinely impressed by people living good Christian lives, they also misunderstood things here and there, which led them to humility, if in a humorous way.

A family had come to visit the monastery and stay the night. When two of the sisters were making the beds in the large guest room for the family, the mother told them, "Don't go to all that trouble."

"No, no, it's no trouble," the nuns responded.

"No, really, we brought sheets with us," the woman said.

"You did? Why did you do that? You didn't have to do that!" the nuns told her.

"It doesn't matter. We didn't want to bother you," she said.

"Okay, well, how many pillows would you like, then?" they asked.

"We don't need any, thank you," she responded.

"What you do mean? You don't even want one?"

"No, thank you," she answered.

"Not even for the children?" the nuns asked.

"No, that's okay. We'll just take a few blankets," she said, gesturing to the folded blankets in the open cupboard. After handing her a blanket for each family member, the two nuns walked away amazed.

"They don't even use pillows! We're monastics and use pillows, and here a whole family comes to visit us and they don't even use pillows! We're useless. We're worse than all!" They were mortified, thinking this family practiced such strict asceticism while they used pillows for the four hours of sleep they got. They mentioned this to the other sisters as well as to Sr. Irene, who knew the family personally. Later, when she saw the teenaged son, she asked, "Your mom told the sisters you wouldn't be needing pillows. Do you not sleep with a pillow?" she asked.

"Of course I do! We all do. My mom just didn't want to make work for the sisters by dirtying any sheets or pillowcases, so she brought them all with us—including pillows."

When I heard this, I must admit I laughed pretty hard. The nuns, in their goodness, were put to shame thinking they were dirt compared to this family. It is such a perfect example of their pure innocence; no cynicism or skepticism could be found in them. They accepted everything with simplicity and an open heart, a quality that helped them be humbled by others, even when it was rooted in a misunderstanding.

There were also times when the sisters were legitimately impressed by people in the world. Gregory, a young struggling Christian in the world, made an impact on one of the sisters.

She was moved to hear that he kept his oil lamp lit all day and all night, burning in front of his icon corner. Every evening he censed his whole house and outside the front door. Once he told her, "I don't always have time to read the full Akathist hymn to the Mother of God every day. Do you know what prayers I can say at the end of the day if I have missed it? You know, to make up for it?"

Hearing this question, the nun was very humbled by this young man. He worked full time, was married, and had two young children. And yet he was grieved that he sometimes failed to complete the prayers he tried to say each day.

We can find examples in many places of good Christians living a life of prayer and fasting in the world. We can find similar or greater examples in a monastery. In each case we can learn from them and be humbled by them.

The monastics are a light for us, but as it turns out, we can often shed a little light for them. In their humility they always see the struggle and fruit of someone else's labor as being far greater than their own. We should do likewise. Seeing the good fruit of others, we should strive to be humbled and inspired.

SCENT of HOLINESS

Prophesy, O Son of Man, to These Dry Bones

ONE MILD AND SUNNY FALL afternoon, John and I went to the monastery's garden, with my brother and sister-in-law, to visit Sr. Nektaria. She had wanted to take us to the cemetery to see the ossuary and the old chapel. But first she gave us a tour around the garden, wanting us to see the fruit of the sisters' prayers and labors. She showed us the different little greenhouses and pointed out the vegetables in season. She told us her plans to plant bushes along the pathway so the flowers would make the space more beautiful, and she took us into the little hut she had in the garden where she could have some water or a snack when she needed it.

Afterward, we made our way down the small hill to the graveyard. Two graves were open, waiting for the next two nuns the Lord would decide to take from this life. There were only four graves in the whole graveyard. The reason for this is a practical one.

In Greece, after someone has been buried for three years, their remains are dug up and placed in an ossuary, if at a monastery, or in a mausoleum* if in the city. Land is generally limited, so when a person dies, they open a grave, take out the remains, and place the recently deceased inside. Ossuaries at monasteries usually hold thousands of bones.

The ossuary at this monastery had never been properly organized. Throughout the years, every nun who died was merely placed in a crypt, more reminiscent of a hole than of a room. The ossuary itself was located above the crypt, underneath the chapel, at ground level with the graveyard.

When this sisterhood came to restore the monastery, they took out each bone and skull, cleaned them one by one, and neatly placed all the skulls on shelves and the bones into containers.

Sr. Nektaria opened the door to the ossuary for us. Entering, she turned on the lights to reveal some three hundred skulls lining the walls. In the corner was a large icon of the Resurrection of our Lord with a censer in front of it.

"I cense the bones every day while chanting *Hristos Anesti*," she told us.

"Come in here," she said, gesturing to an open doorway leading into a smaller room. "There's more in here."

This room was about one-quarter of the size of the main room and had a lower ceiling. She pointed to a hole in the floor and said, "That's the crypt, where all the bones were kept until we took them out.

"Here are some incorrupt parts we found. Of course we don't know whom they belong to, but there's an arm and a hand. Over here are a few skulls that look as though they belonged to children. We're not sure who they were or when they died. Now come and let me show you this . . ."

Back in the main ossuary, she walked over to one of the shelves and said, "Do you notice how on every skull there are three lines, one on either side of the skull, going down from the center toward the ear sockets, and one going straight back?"

"Yes," we answered.

"Well, a skull that belongs to a hieromonk has one more line. It goes down the front onto the forehead, making the sign of the cross. We know some hieromonks were also buried here, and these are their skulls," she said gesturing to the section of the shelving closest to the door.

"I don't know if this miracle happens to all priests or just those who are also monastics, but in any case, it's quite something," she said, tracing her finger over the line on one of the skulls that had this unique marking.

"And come and see this," she said, walking back into the smaller room.

But I didn't follow with the rest. I stayed in the main ossuary. Staring at all those skulls with their empty sockets staring back at me, I thought of the day of the final Resurrection.

Someday we'll arise—whether it's to eternal life or to eternal death, in either case we will return to our bodies, I thought to myself.

And looking around at all those dry bones, I thought of them being drawn back together, bound up by ligaments, muscles, flesh. Reflecting on this, my mind naturally turned to the Prophet Ezekiel:

And He said to me, "Son of man, can these bones live?"
So I answered, "O Lord God, You know."
Again He said to me, "Prophesy to these bones, and say to them, 'O dry bones, hear the word of the Lord! Thus says the Lord God to these bones: "Surely I will cause breath to enter into you, and you shall live. I will put sinews on you and bring flesh upon you, cover you with skin and put breath in you; and you shall live. Then you shall know that I *am* the Lord."'"
(Ezekiel 37:3–6)

I reached out to touch one of the skulls, and to my surprise my hand pulled back involuntarily just as my fingers were about to touch the bone. I resisted my hesitancy, stretched out my hand once more, and laid it on one of the skulls.

KNOT THIRTY-TWO

This was a person. She had hopes and dreams, struggles and hardships just as I do. She thought up thousands of thoughts in that very skull, but now, no longer. She lies dead, her soul having long ago departed from her bones, and she awaits the Final Judgment. I wonder who she was, what she was like. How old she was when she died.

Before I know it, I will also die, and only a pile of bones will remain. And who will remember me? Once those around me who knew me pass out of this life, I too will be forgotten. I will cease to exist in this world.

As I reflected thus, my eyes began to fill with tears. Coming out of the other room, Sr. Nektaria looked at me. Turning toward one of the skulls, she knocked on it with her knuckle: "This is all we are, Constantina, dry bones—nothing."

She looked as though she were about to cry, and I couldn't hold back my tears.

Just then John, Matthew, and Catherine came back into the main ossuary, and we sang *Christ is Risen*. We sang for all those souls that had departed. We sang with the hope that we would all one day rise with Him. We sang with the conviction that to live for Christ is to die to self—that if we, like Christ, are to be victorious, we must also trample down death by death.

Finishing, we each venerated the large icon of the Resurrection and exited. Coming out into the sun, I think we all felt a little somber, but also a little more determined to keep that image of death ever before us. For in the not-so-distant future, our own bodies will join those dry bones in their destitution, their loneliness, their soullessness—hopefully, only to have the Spirit breathed back into us for the resurrection of eternal life.

KNOT THIRTY-THREE

Only the Furnace Isn't Good

A FAMILY, WHO HAD TRAVELED three or four hours from their village to visit Elder Isidoros, were waiting for him in the reception room, so I went to get him. Once I told him the family had arrived, he was in such a hurry to go and speak with them that he didn't even want to take the time to wash his hands after working with the vegetables.

While I escorted him across the courtyard to the building where the family was waiting, I described our surroundings to him. "Be careful, there's a flower pot to your right. The flowers in it are very beautiful." Now, the Greek word I used was *oraia*, which can mean both "beautiful" and "good."

"Everything is good, everything is good. Only the furnace isn't good," he responded. He used the word "furnace" as most Greeks do when speaking of hell.

"And it's only into the furnace that I don't want to go," I told him.

"You won't, if you struggle. As long as someone struggles, they won't go into the furnace. Tell me, do you obey Fr. Luke?" he asked.

"I try, Papouli, but I don't obey like I should," I said, helping him up the stairs.

"That's okay, do what you can. So long as you are at least *trying* to obey," he told me, patting my hand.

To me, the elder was a true struggling Christian: a true, obedient, spiritual child. That's why he worked countless miracles—all due to his humble disposition and unfaltering faith. May we strive to imitate his Christian virtues, especially his obedience and his humility!

Old Hands and Young Faces

SINCE NUNS ARE COVERED IN BLACK, there is not much you see of them other than their hands and faces. But these reveal their whole life to you. In my experience, nuns' faces are extraordinarily young-looking. They often look many years younger than they are.

The first time I saw an Orthodox nun, she looked strange to me. I think it was primarily because we rarely see a woman without makeup, and because her entire forehead was covered by her headscarf. It didn't take long, though, before I started to see how much beauty was contained in a nun's face. They have a naturally pleasant appearance that has long passed away from our contemporary world.

Nuns' hands, however, are entirely the opposite. They almost always look old and worn out—revealing manual labor, sometimes cut and usually scarred.

Once I burnt my thumb on a frying pan. "I hope it scars,

because then I would look more like the nuns," I told my husband, laughing.

Unlike their faces, their hands look about thirty years older than they are.

I mentioned this to Sr. Raphaela once and she said, "Our hands look old because of the work. Our faces look young because we don't wear makeup."

That is partially true; makeup is very predominant in our contemporary world but can age a face considerably. However, I believe their faces also hold traces of the purity that dwells in their hearts.

Night and day they labor in prayer and work to purify their hearts in order to make them suitable dwelling places of the Holy Spirit. Night and day they struggle to bow down and accept the difficult weight of monastic obedience. Night and day they fight themselves, their thoughts, their feelings, their self-pity and self-justification. Night and day they take up their cross and, with their gaze fixed on Christ, they lay down their life for Him. I saw this in their faces.

I stood beside them in work and prayer for countless hours. I learned from their patience, their struggle, and their self-sacrifice. Their faces contained the serenity that comes from death to self. Each of them on her own individual level had become a vessel of the Most Holy Trinity, and their faces revealed this.

After years of visiting them, working with them, praying with them, laughing and crying with them, my hands still look soft and young and my face worn and old. However, I hold onto the hope that someday, through their prayers, I will catch up with them and finally accomplish what I have, haphazardly, been attempting for years—to die to myself in order to live for Christ.

KNOT THIRTY-THREE

We Live in Order to Learn How to Die

I WAS LYING IN BED, still awake, when I heard the telephone ring. It was around one-thirty in the morning, and we had celebrated the Feast of the Life-giving and saving Cross that morning in church.

I heard my husband say, "Oh Sarah, it's you. Oh she did, did she . . ." That's when I knew. "Markella," I said aloud.

"I know it's late, but I needed to call now because the funeral will be tomorrow morning at eleven. I don't know if you'll be able to arrive in time, but at least this way you know," she told me.

"I'm glad you called. God willing, we'll be there," I said.

Strangely, I had been thinking a lot about death those last few days, about how sad it is that we are separated from those we love. And here it was the day we celebrate Christ's victory over death by His death on the Cross, and I was learning of my dear, sweet Sr. Markella's own death.

I shed a few tears but felt a calm sweetness.

Bravo, I thought. *You did it! You finished the race!*

I don't believe she could have died on a better day. Having suffered so much in her life, her dying on the Sunday of the Cross was confirmation to me that she suffered like a martyr.

With difficulty I fell back asleep, and the next morning hurried to get to the train station. We arrived at the monastery to see the gate wide open. They were about twenty minutes into the funeral, and as I was walking across the courtyard I could hear the sisters chanting.

I entered the church to find it full of people holding burning candles. I made my way through the crowd to get as close as possible. My sister-in-law handed me a candle, and I joined its wick with another woman's burning candle. The whole church was illuminated by the warm light of burning candles. It looked and felt like an intimate Paschal celebration.

The local bishop, six priests, and two deacons stood in a semicircle facing Sr. Markella. Her sons and seven grandsons stood to her right, her daughters and one granddaughter to her left. I recognized them since I had met most of them throughout my years of visiting the monastery.

Since the priests and sisters were chanting back and forth, I assumed they had reached the part of the funeral service in which the *idiomela* are chanted. These hymns are chanted in the eight tones, highlighting with the alternation of joyful and sorrowful melodies the mixture of emotions one goes through when encountering the death of a faithful Christian.

Before I knew it, it was time for the final greeting. The abbess went first, the nuns followed behind, and each kissed the icon of the Resurrection that rested on top of Sr. Markella's chest. Then each kissed her face and said goodbye. I am certain that this was the hardest part for everyone in attendance. I don't know if anyone managed to avoid shedding tears. How do you say goodbye to someone you know and love? How does one accept the unnaturalness of death?

I approached her and venerated the icon. I knelt down and through tears, kissed her forehead. "Goodbye, Markella," I said, then got up and waited for the rest to bid her farewell. Then two sisters pulled the cloth—embroidered with the great schema—that covered her body up over her head and sewed it closed.

The sisters waited outside with two processional fans and a cross, chanting. Each held a candle and waited while Sr. Markella's grandsons lifted up the funeral bier and began exiting the church. The nuns led the way with the bishop, priests, and deacons following behind. Sr. Markella was carried behind them, and the people followed after her.

I spotted Mrs. Dina in the crowd and hurried to greet her. It had been a few years since we last saw each other. She had grown up with Sr. Markella and was understandably grieved to see her depart. In fact, almost everyone I had ever met at the monastery was there that day. It felt like a great big family reunion, and I was overwhelmingly grateful that God had allowed me to be a member of such a wonderful family.

Processing with everyone else, we stopped just before we went down the little hill into the graveyard, and the nuns traded places with Sr. Markella's grandsons. Just as in life, so in death Sr. Markella left behind her earthly family for her spiritual family; her earthly family stepped aside while her spiritual family bore her to her final resting place.

At the graveside the sisters gathered around the open tomb. I stood across from them next to Sr. Paraskevi's grave. As the bishop began the Trisagion* prayers, the sisters brought the funeral bier to the edge of the grave.

Srs. Akakia and Seraphima stood in the grave and received her body, which to everyone's surprise was still flexible. Rigor mortis had not set in, and never would. I am told this is a gift from God to great-schema monastics. They laid her in the grave, placed a cement slab just above her head, and climbed out. This way they make sure her skull is not crushed by the weight of the earth.

During all of this, the sisters had no place to put down the pillow that Sr. Markella's head had rested on, nor the bottle of oil, or Sr. Akakia's *exorasso,** so they handed them all to me to hold. Although stuff was piled up in my arms, making it difficult to participate, I felt honored to help Sr. Markella one last time, to assist the sisterhood in completing a very important task.

While the hot sun shone down on us, the bishop said the final prayers and I heard one of the sisters begin *Christos anesti* (Christ is risen).

Everyone joined in. Here we were in the middle of Great Lent and yet proclaiming the hope of the Resurrection. It, of course, drew my mind to the epistle we had heard during the service: "And the dead in Christ will rise first. Then we who are alive *and* remain shall be caught up together with them in the clouds to meet the Lord in the air. And thus we shall always be with the Lord" (1 Thess. 4:16–17).

After the Di'evhon, Sr. Euphemia said, "Master and Lord, grant rest to your servant," one hundred times while all the sisters crossed themselves at each petition. Then, one by one, starting with the abbess, we each threw down a handful of dirt on Sr. Markella's body.

"I knew her soul had departed, but it was strange to throw dirt on Markella's body," Sr. Sarah confided in me afterward.

The workers helped Sr. Seraphima cover the rest of Sr. Markella's body with slabs of cement and fill in the grave with dirt. Before heading back to the monastery to eat *kolyva** and the sweets the sisters had prepared, the people went into the ossuary to venerate the Resurrection icon and see the remains of those who had gone before us. The scene was appropriately reminiscent of one of the hymns the sisters had chanted during Sr. Markella's funeral:

I called to mind the Prophet who shouted,
"I am but earth and ash."
And once again I looked with attention on the tombs,
and I saw the bones therein which of flesh were naked;
and I said, "Which indeed is he that is king? Or which is soldier?
Which is the wealthy, which the needy?
Which the righteous, or which the sinner?"
But to Your servant, O Lord, grant that with the righteous
she may repose.

And that is all we can hope to receive from death—that with the righteous we may all repose. This is the monastic life: spending your whole life focused on learning how to die well. Their gaze is ever fixed on death, knowing that if this life is lived properly, then death is merely the beginning of new life, true life.

I pray with all my strength, with all my heart, mind, and soul that we be accounted worthy to "serve Him without fear, / In holiness and righteousness before Him all the days of our life" (Luke 1:74–75), together with the angels, the saints, and the Most Holy Lady, the ever-virgin Mary, unto the ages and ages. Amen.

For if we died with *Him*,
We shall also live with *Him*.
If we endure,
We shall also reign with *Him*.
(2 Tim. 2:11–12)

Therefore, let us leave all the sweet pleasures of the world, as false and short-lived, that we may inherit what is true and ageless. —St. Irene Chrysovolandou

EPILOGUE

SINCE BECOMING ORTHODOX—and especially while living in Greece—I have received numerous blessings. I have met living saints, visited holy sites, and venerated countless holy relics of ascetics, martyrs, virgins, and hierarchs. All of this the Lord has allowed me to experience for the benefit of my hardened heart and the enlightening of my darkened mind.

Instead of keeping these wonderful experiences to myself, I decided I would try to distribute my blessings. I may not gain much more than the one talent that was entrusted to me, but *The Scent of Holiness* was my attempt to at least put my talent "in the bank" so the Master would receive his own with interest (Matt. 25:28).

Persuaded by the following vision, St. Gregory Palamas, the Archbishop of Thessaloniki, decided to share his own talent by writing about the divine wisdom he received:

In his third year at St. Savvas, while Gregory was immersed in holy mental prayer, it seems a light sleep took hold of him;

and then he beheld the following vision. It appeared to him that in his hands there was a vessel of pure milk, so full that it was flowing over the brim. This same milk then turned to the most excellent wine which emitted a wonderful fragrance. So abundantly did it flow that both his hands and garments were doused and penetrated by the marvelous fragrance. As soon as St. Gregory perceived the scent, he was filled with holy joy. Then there appeared unto him a radiant youth, who said: "Why dost thou not share this overflowing and wonderful drink with others? Why hast thou left it to pour forth to no use? Dost thou not know that this is the gift of God and that when poured out it is inexhaustible?" Gregory then asked, "Yet, what if there are no people who worthily seek it or even ask for it?" The angel answered, "Though presently there are none that seek this with desire, nonetheless, thou shalt do thy duty and not speculate in thought or neglect to distribute it. Thou must render unto the Master the talent entrusted to thee. Thou dost precisely know the command and the talent that was given to the unprofitable servant and what became of him!" The angel then departed, leaving Gregory enveloped in light, sitting for many hours, pondering the matter.[16]

Although I have nothing to offer that could ever compare to St. Gregory Palamas's contribution to the Church, I felt the need to share the experiences I had stored up in my heart (Luke 2:19). St. Gregory received and recorded *divine* wisdom, acquired through his asceticism and holiness. The milk in my own miniature and insignificant cup is not mine, but rather a collection of the surplus of overflowing cups belonging to others.

But in applying my heart to instruction (Prov. 23:12), and in looking upon the nourishing drink I had been given, I felt the need to share such spiritual sweetness. Of course my one talent is nothing compared with the countless talents belonging to the holy persons I have met. But, unable to find a better way to multiply that which was entrusted to me, I labored to offer my fellow struggling Christian brothers and sisters a small gift—a taste of the blessed and fragrant wine poured out for me in that holy Orthodox country called Greece.

Finally, in the words of St. John of the Ladder, I too "am full aware, my good friends, that the struggles I described shall seem to some incredible, [while] to others hard to believe. . . . But to the courageous soul, they shall go away carrying zeal in their hearts."[17]

I wish for you all to be filled with this zeal, a well-informed and firmly established zeal, that will lead to as great or greater deeds than those described in this book. And pray for me so that I too might come to imitate the Christ-centered life I have described in these pages.

Glory be to God!

ENDNOTES

1   See Saint John Climacus, *The Ladder of Divine Ascent*, trans. Norman Russell (Paulist Press: New Jersey, 1982), p. 234.

2   My husband was ordained to the diaconate during our last year living in Greece.

3   Saint John Chrysostom, *Pros piston patera (To the faithful father)*, J.P. Migne, ed., 3, 14, PG47, pp. 372–374.

4   Archimandrite Sophrony, *St. Silouan the Athonite*, trans. Rosemary Edmonds (St. Vladimir Seminary Press: New York, 1999), pp. 407–408.

5   Abba Dorotheos, "On the Fear of God," in *Practical Teaching on the Christian Life*, trans. Constantine Scouteris (University of Athens: Athens, 2002), p. 113.

6   Saint Nikodemos the Hagiorite, *Exomologetarion: A Manuel of Confession*, trans. George Dokos (Uncut Mountain Press: Greece, 2006), p. 288.

7   Saint Syncletike, "Life and Struggles of Syncletike of Alexandria: On Asceticism," in *The Lives of the Spiritual Mothers: An Orthodox Materikon of Women Monastics and Ascetics*, trans. and compiled by Holy Apostles Convent (Holy Apostles Convent: Colorado, 1991), p. 49.

8   Abba Arsenios, *Ευεργεντινος*, vol. 4 (Bishop Matthew Laggi of Oinoi: Athens, 1997), p. 366.

9 Metropolitan Augustine Kantiotis of Florena, Κοσμάς ο Αιτωλός (*Cosmas the Aetolian*), (Stavros: Athens, 2005), pp. 155–156.

10 Elder Joseph, *Monastic Wisdom: The Letters of Elder Joseph the Hesychast*, trans. Ephraim Poonen (Saint Anthony's Greek Orthodox Monastery: Arizona, 1999), p. 48.

11 Elder Paisios the Hagiorite, Πνευματική Αφυπνίση (*Spiritual Awakening*), vol. 2 (Saint John the Evangelist and Theologian Hesychastarion: Thessaloniki, 1999), pp. 148–149.

12 Elder Porphyrios of Athens, *Wounded by Love: The Life and Wisdom of Elder Porphyrios*, trans. John Raffan (Denise Harvey: Evia, 2005), p. 215.

13 Saint Basil the Great, "Concerning Envy," in *Fathers of the Church: Saint Basil: Ascetical Works (A New Translation)*, trans. Lugwig Schopp, vol. 9 (The Catholic University of America Press, 1962), pp. 469–470.

14 It is the practice in some Orthodox countries to observe a Lenten-style fast for twenty-four hours before receiving Holy Communion.

15 Saint Theophan the Recluse, "What to Do about a Bad Priest," in *The Letters of St. Theophan the Recluse*, trans. Fr. Justin Brian Frederick, accessed July 4, 2012, http://www.stmaximus.org/files/Documents/BadPriest.htm.

16 Holy Apostles Convent, *The Lives of the Pillars of Orthodoxy: Saints Photios of Constantinople, Gregory Palamas, and Mark of Ephesus* (Holy Apostles Convent: Colorado, 1997), p. 208.

17 Saint John Climacus, *The Ladder of Divine Ascent*, trans. Norman Russell (Paulist Press: New Jersey, 1982), p. 27.

GLOSSARY

Acrostic   A form of poetry or other writing in which the first letters of the lines or stanzas spell out a word or message. In the case of Akathist* hymns, it follows alphabetical order.

Akathist   A hymn of twenty-four stanzas honoring a saint, the Mother of God, the Holy Trinity, or a holy event.

Analavos   Greek for "to take on" or "to bear." In the context of the monastic schema or habit, it signifies the taking up of the cross (Luke 9:23) by the monk or nun. It is a garment worn around the neck that covers the front and may reach the knees. It looks similar to a priest's stole and in the Greek tradition is embroidered in color, predominantly red.

Antidoron   Literally "instead of the gifts." The bread that is distributed to the faithful following the dismissal of the Divine Liturgy.

Archimandrite   A title bestowed on a hieromonk* as a sign of respect or gratitude for service to the Church. It is similar to the title *archpriest* given to married clergy.

Ascesis   The Christian struggle to keep the commandments of Christ. In the context of this book, it is used to denote the spiritual struggle against the passions.*

Ascetic   One who practices strict ascesis.*

Asceticism   Acts of ascesis.* These include but are not limited to fasting, prayer, shedding tears over one's sins, good works, and general denial of one's self-will.

Athos   Mount Athos, or the Holy Mountain, is a self-governed men's monastic community on a peninsula in Northern Greece.

Belt of the Mother of God   According to Tradition, the Apostle Thomas was the only apostle absent from the Dormition (falling asleep) of the Mother of God. He was grieved to learn of this, but suddenly found himself witnessing the Virgin's ascent to heaven. He pleaded with her to give him a blessing; she untied her belt (made of camel skins) and gave it to him. This belt is the only existing relic of the Virgin Mary. Its only known remaining piece is housed at the Holy Monastery of Vatopedi on Mount Athos.* The Orthodox Church celebrates the Holy Belt of the Theotokos on August 31. As a blessing, the Fathers lay pieces of cord or rope across the relic and give them out to the faithful—particularly women who desire to conceive—to wear around their waist.

Bless   In addition to its regular meaning, this word is used by monastics to mean "forgive me," "hello," or "good-bye."

Blessing   Besides its usual meaning, a "blessing" can also mean permission given for a particular action.

Canon of St. Andrew of Crete   A canon is a long hymn divided into nine odes, each ode consisting of numerous stanzas. The canon of St. Andrew is prayed during Great Lent.

Catechumen   One who receives instruction on the principles of the Christian faith while preparing for holy baptism.

Cell   The personal living space of a monastic.

Cenobitic   From the Greek words *koinos bios* (common life), cenobitic (as an adjective) refers to a monastery in which the monastics own all things in common.

Clean Monday   The first Monday in Great Lent, which begins the Lenten fasting period and signifies the leaving behind of one's sinful ways.

Compline   The second service of the day (following Vespers*). It is said sometime in the evening; the Greek word for this is *apoodeipnon*, literally, "after dinner."

Despota   The Greek word for "Master." *Despota* is the way Greek Orthodox faithful greet their bishop.

Diakonema   A monastic's assigned job at a monastery. In English the word "obedience" is often used for this.

Di'evhon   Literally, "through the prayers." Usually refers to the title of the common prayer, "Through the prayers of our holy fathers, O Lord Jesus Christ, have mercy on us."

Diskos   A footed plate used for the eucharistic bread.

Elder   A hieromonk, priest, or monk who, ideally, has reached a state of purity by the grace of God. In a broader sense, though, it is used as a respectful title for any spiritual father, elderly hieromonk, priest, or monk.

Epitrachelion   A liturgical stole worn by bishops and priests.

Evlogeite   The Greek imperative of the word meaning "bless." See *bless* for a fuller definition.

Evlogisan   See *bless*.

Exorasso   A long, black garment worn on top of a monastic's or priest's clothing.

Forgiveness Sunday   The last day of the Triodion* season and the day immediately prior to Clean Monday.* In the evening a Vespers* service is celebrated, after which it is customary to seek and offer forgiveness within one's parish community.

Geronda   (Pronounced "yeh´-ron-da"). See *elder*.

Gerontissa   (Pronounced "yeh´-ron-di-sa"). Used as a respectful title for any abbess or older nun.

Great Feasts   There are twelve major feasts in the Orthodox Church's liturgical calendar. Five of those feasts are in honor of historical events directly relating to the Mother of God, while the remaining seven are in honor of historical events in the life of the Lord Jesus Christ. Pascha* is not numbered in the twelve as it is considered the "feast of feasts."

Great Schema   The schema, usually called the "great schema" or "angelic schema," is the habit of a monastic who has attained the highest level of monasticism. It is called the "angelic schema" because its bearer strives to live angelically in purity and devotion to God alone.

Heart   The heart is not simply the physical organ but the spiritual center of man's being. The spiritual heart is located in the physical heart and is the center of man's human and spiritual self. Prayer of the heart constitutes prayer of the whole person: mind, soul, spirit, and body.

Hermitage   The cell or small home of a hermit and his brotherhood, if he has one.

Hesychast   One who practices *hesychia*, the ascetical practice of noetic stillness linked with watchfulness and deepened by the unceasing Jesus Prayer.

Hesychastarion   A monastery usually under its own jurisdiction or that of another monastery, as opposed to being under a particular local bishop.

Holy Gifts   The consecrated bread and wine of the Eucharist.

Holy Mountain   See *Athos*.

Hours   A group of four services either spaced throughout the day or grouped together and done at the same time.

Iconology   The study of the theology of icons.

Iconostasis   Icon screen—a wall of icons separating the sanctuary from the nave in an Orthodox temple.

Ison   Greek for "equal." The drone accompaniment to Byzantine chant. It can be chanted either on the syllable "oo" or using the words of the hymn.

Jesus Prayer   The Jesus Prayer is a short prayer that is continually repeated, addressed to the Person of Jesus Christ: "Lord Jesus Christ, have mercy on me." It is also said in its longer version: "Lord Jesus Christ, Son of God, have mercy on me, a sinner."

Hieromonk   A monk who is also a priest.

Katzio   A large silver hand-censer.

Kolyva   A ritual food consisting of boiled wheat (in the Greek tradition). It is made for the service of prayers for the departed or in honor of a saint. After the priest blesses it, it is served to those who attended the service.

Komboskini   A prayer rope—a cord with many knots used in prayer to help the mind concentrate. At each knot, one prayer is said.

Leave-taking   The final day of a festal season.

Logismoi   The nominative plural form of the Greek word *logismos; logismous* is the accusative plural form. Literally, "thoughts." In the patristic sense, "thoughts" refer not only to thoughts in the ordinary sense, but also to evil thoughts provoked by the demons.

Matins   A service of prayer usually celebrated prior to the Divine Liturgy. As its name suggests, it is intended to be served in the morning, but may also be served late at night as a vigil. It consists of psalms, canons, and hymns.

Mausoleum   A building that houses tombs or bones of the deceased.

Memorial   A service in which the priest commemorates and prays for the deceased. Traditionally, it is done on any day of the week except Sundays. On Sunday the Lord's Resurrection is celebrated; thus the Church decided prayers for the dead on this particular day were not fitting.

Metanoia   In its primary sense, *metanoia* (pronounced "meh-tah´-nee-ah") means "repentance," literally a "change of mind." However, it can also refer to the specific act of making the sign of the cross, followed by a bow either to the ground or to the waist. It is a gesture of reverence, worship, respect, or repentance. A typical prayer rule includes a number of *metanoies* done while saying the Jesus Prayer. Sometimes the word "prostration" is used in its place.

Name Day   The celebration of a particular person whose name corresponds to the saint or liturgical feast celebrated that day in the church calendar. For many Orthodox Christians, this day takes precedence over birthday celebrations.

Narthex   The first room one enters in an Orthodox temple. Traditionally, it is the place where those unable to receive the Eucharist—non-Orthodox, the possessed, those repenting of a serious sin, and after a certain point in the Divine Liturgy, those learning the faith (catechumens*)—stand during services.

Noetic   Belonging to, characteristic of, or perceptible to the *nous*, which is often, though inaccurately, translated in English as "intellect." The Fathers mainly refer to the nous as the soul and the heart. More specifically, it constitutes the innermost aspect of the heart. However, the nous is more commonly known as the energy of the soul, whereas the heart is the essence of the soul.

Panagia   A Greek title for the Virgin Mary, meaning "all-holy one." It is used as an affectionate name for the Mother of God by many Orthodox faithful.

Pantocrator   A Greek title given to Jesus Christ which means "ruler of all."

Papouli   A Greek diminutive of "priest," also used as an affectionate title for older monks who are not priests.

Paraclesis   From the Greek meaning "supplication" or "request." It is also the name of the Orthodox supplication service, which is comprised of various psalms, prayers, and a canon.

Pascha   The Orthodox word for Easter, taken from the Hebrew word for "Passover."

Passion   A spiritual disease that dominates the soul. When one repeatedly falls into a certain sin, it becomes second nature—a passion.

Philotimo   Literally "love of honor." The Christian desire to do good for the sake of doing good, and not as a means to a reward. It is an act or state of being of selfless love.

The Prayer   The Jesus Prayer* is often referred to simply as "the prayer."

Prayer rope   See *komboskini*.

Prayer of the heart   The highest form of prayer, in which the mind is kept in the heart by the grace of the Holy Spirit and prays there without distraction.

Presvytera   A title given to a priest's wife, taken from the Greek word *presbyter*.

Presanctified Liturgy   A Presanctified Liturgy is only celebrated on weekdays in Great Lent. Since the Church does not celebrate the Resurrection of Christ in Great Lent, except on weekends, a portion of Holy Communion is kept for the weekday liturgies during the fast. The order of the service is also different from that of the Divine Liturgy.

Prozimi   Although *prozimi* is simply the Greek word for "yeast" or "leaven," in this book the word signifies the specific, miraculous leaven used by the sisters in *prosphora** recipes.

Proskomidi   *Proskomidi* is a service of preparation for the Divine Liturgy in which the portion of bread to be used for the Eucharist is cut out of the *prosphora,** and during which the names of living and dead Orthodox Christians are commemorated.

Prosphora   A *prosphoron* (plural: *prosphora*) is a round loaf of bread specially prepared to be used in the Proskomidi* in preparation for the Divine Liturgy.

Royal Doors   A set of doors located in the middle of the iconostasis leading into the sanctuary. Only ordained clergy are permitted to enter and exit through them.

Sacristan   The person in charge of looking after the needs of the church building.

Schema   See Great Schema.

Skete   A small monastic village, usually consisting of a central church and several cells.*

Stasidi   *Stasidia* (plural of *stasidi*) are large throne-like chairs that line the walls in most churches in Greece. They are usually connected in a row. The stasidi has a seat, which often folds up, so one can either stand on the small wooden platform below or sit on the seat. The former allows one to rest, but in an almost standing position. The stasidi has armrests for both positions.

Symantron   A shaped strip of metal that is hung outside a monastery church and is hit rhythmically with a metal instrument before the services to call the faithful to prayer.

Synaxis   The Greek word for "gathering" or "congregation." It is used to signify a meeting among a group of people (usually of like mind).

Talanton   A long wooden plank that is either hung outside a monastery church or held by a monastic. Before a church service begins, a monastic rhythmically knocks on it with a wooden hammer. Oral and pictorial tradition tells us this is how Noah called the animals to enter the ark. Like the animals, we are drawn by the sound to enter the "ark of our salvation," the Church.

Theotokos   A title confirmed in the Third Ecumenical Council for the Virgin Mary, meaning "God-bearer."

Tonsure   The rite in which a novice becomes a monk or nun. It is called a tonsure because during the rite, some of the novice's hair is cut.

Trapeza   Ancient Greek for "dining hall." In contemporary use it refers only to a monastery's dining hall.

Triodion   A three-week liturgical time period preceding Great Lent in which the Church and her faithful prepare for the forty-day fast.

Trisagion   A combination of the Greek words meaning "three" and "holy." It is the title of the Orthodox hymn, "Holy God, Holy Mighty, Holy Immortal, have mercy on us," which is always said or sung three times.

Troparion   A short hymn or stanza sung in Orthodox services.

GLOSSARY

Vespers   A service of evening prayer.

Watchfulness   The practice of paying close attention to one's thoughts, intentions, and emotions. The aim is to resist temptation and impure thoughts so as to keep a constant state of remembrance of God.

Yia-yia   A Greek diminutive for "grandmother."

ABOUT THE AUTHOR

CONSTANTINA R. PALMER is originally from New Brunswick, a quaint province on Canada's Atlantic coast. Currently, however, she lives in Thessaloniki, Greece, with her husband, a deacon in the Canadian Archdiocese of the OCA. She has called Greece home for five years, in which time she has received her Master's degree in Theology from the Aristotle University of Thessaloniki.  She is also an iconographer and a student of Byzantine chant.

Ancient Faith Ministries hopes you have enjoyed and benefited from this book. The proceeds from the sales of our books only partially cover the costs of operating our nonprofit ministry—which includes both the work of Ancient Faith Publishing (formerly Conciliar Press) and the work of Ancient Faith Radio. Your financial support makes it possible to continue this ministry both in print and online. Donations are tax-deductible and can be made at www.ancientfaith.com.

ANCIENT FAITH RADIO

Internet-Based Orthodox Radio:
Podcasts, 24-hour music and talk stations,
teaching, conference recordings, and much more,
at www.ancientfaith.com

OTHER BOOKS OF INTEREST

A Book of Hours
Meditations on the Traditional Christian Hours of Prayer
by Patricia Colling Egan

Eastern and Western Christians share a rich spiritual heritage in the Hours of Prayer—the brief services of praise and psalmody that mark the progress of each day, sanctifying the hours of our lives. In this gem of a book, Patricia Egan digs deeply into the meaning of each of the Hours, drawing on poetry, nature, experience, and theology to show how the services reflect the different aspects of our salvation and our lives. *A Book of Hours* is an excellent companion for anyone who wants to experience the blessing of praying through the Hours of each day.

Inside pages are printed in two colors, and feature calligraphy elements.

• Paperback, 192 pages (ISBN: 978-1-936270-06-4) AFP Order No. 008076—$21.95*

Community of Grace
An Orthodox Christian Year in Alaska
by Mary Alice Cook

Throughout the Christian world and beyond, people are beginning to recognize the need for community—the need to belong to a close and caring group of people who provide each other with physical, material, emotional, and spiritual support on a daily basis. But many are floundering in their attempts to create this kind of community.

Community of Grace is not a textbook for creating community. Rather, it's the story of one successful community, made up of the stories of the people who made it happen, and told in the context of the Orthodox worship that binds them all together.

Includes a 16-page photo section.

• Paperback, 208 pages (ISBN: 978-1-936270-07-1) AFP Order No. 008077—$17.95*

At the Corner of East and Now
A Modern Life in Ancient Christian Orthodoxy
by Frederica Mathewes-Green

Acclaimed author Frederica Mathewes-Green takes us through a typical Divine Liturgy in her little parish of Holy Cross in Baltimore, setting of her well-loved book *Facing East.* Interspersed with reflections on the liturgy and the Orthodox faith are accounts of adventures around the country. In all the places she visits and all the people she meets, Frederica finds insights about faith, American life, and what it means to be human, and she shares these insights with the wit, pathos, and folksy friendliness that have made her one of the most beloved spiritual writers in America.

• Paperback, 270 pages (ISBN: 978-1-888212-34-1) AFP Order No. 007609—$16.95*

Bread & Water, Wine & Oil
An Orthodox Christian Experience of God
by Fr. Meletios Webber

Worry, despair, insecurity, fear of death . . . these are our daily companions. It is precisely where we hurt most that the experience of the Orthodox Church has much to offer. The remedy is not any simple admonitions to fight the good fight, cheer up, or think positively. Rather, the Orthodox method is to change the way we look at the human person (starting with ourselves). Orthodoxy shows us how to "be transformed by the renewing of our mind"—a process that is aided by participation in the traditional ascetic practices and Mysteries of the Church. In this unique and accessible book, Archimandrite Meletios Webber first explores the role of mystery in the Christian life, then walks the reader through the seven major Mysteries (or sacraments) of the Orthodox Church, showing the way to a richer, fuller life in Christ.
• Paperback, 200 pages (ISBN: 978-1-888212-91-4) AFP Order No. 006324—$17.95*

Everywhere Present
Christianity in a One-Storey Universe
by Fr. Stephen Freeman

Have you ever referred to God as "the Man upstairs"? Most Christians living in a secular society have unwittingly relegated God and all things spiritual to the "second storey" of the universe: a realm we cannot reach except through death. The effect of this is to banish God, along with the saints and angels, from our everyday lives.

In *Everywhere Present,* popular blogger and podcaster Fr. Stephen Freeman makes a compelling case for becoming aware of God's living and active presence in every moment of our lives here and now. Learning to practice your Christian faith in a one-storey universe will change your life—and make possible the living, intimate relationship with God you've always dreamed of.
• Paperback, 112 pages (ISBN: 978-1-936270-10-1) AFP Order No. 008102—$12.95*

* Prices do not include applicable sales tax or shipping and handling.
To request a catalog, to obtain complete ordering information, or to place a credit card order, please call Ancient Faith Publishing at (800) 967-7377 or log onto our website: store.ancientfaith.com.